D1414514

The Brontës

MASTERS OF WORLD LITERATURE

PUBLISHED

IN PREPARATION

MASTERS OF WORLD LITERATURE SERIES

LOUIS KRONENBERGER, GENERAL EDITOR

The Brontës

by TOM WINNIFRITH

COLLIER BOOKS
A Division of Macmillan Publishing Co., Inc.
New York

ACKNOWLEDGEMENTS

This book could not have been written without the help of Mrs. Christine Wyman and Mr. Martin Wright. I am also grateful for the advice of Mr. Edward Chitham, Professor Bernard Bergonzi, and Mr. Ray Roberts. The University of Warwick generously gave me one term's sabbatical leave, and I must thank my wife and family for allowing me intervals of peace in which I could write about the Brontës.

Macmillan Publishing Co., Inc.
866 Third Avenue, New York, N.Y. 10022
Collier Macmillan Canada, Ltd.

Library of Congress Cataloging in Publication Data
Winnifrith, Tom.
The Brontës.
(Masters of world literature series)
Bibliography: p.
Includes index.
1. Brontë family. I. Title.
[PR4168.W54 1977b] 823'.8'09 76–47550
ISBN 0–02–007750–5

First Collier Books Edition 1977

This book is also published in a hardcover edition by
Macmillan Publishing Co., Inc.

Printed in the United States of America

To Tabitha

CONTENTS

ABBREVIATIONS

Unless otherwise noted, all references to the novels of the Brontës and to Mrs. Gaskell's *Life of Charlotte Brontë* are to the Haworth edition, edited by Mrs. H. Ward and C. K. Shorter (London, 1899–1900).

AG.   *Agnes Grey.*

BST.   *Brontë Society Transactions.*

EC.   *Essays in Criticism.*

FN.   *Five Novelettes.* Transcribed and edited by W. Gérin (London, 1971).

G.   *The Life of Charlotte Brontë.*

H.   *The Complete Poems of Emily Jane Brontë.* Edited by C. W. Hatfield (London, 1941).

JE.   *Jane Eyre.*

MLR.   *Modern Language Review.*

NCF.   *Nineteenth-Century Fiction.*

P.   *The Professor.*

PMLA.   *Proceedings of the Modern Language Association of America.*

RES.   *Review of English Studies.*

S.   *Shirley.*

SHCBP.   *The Complete Poems of Charlotte Brontë and Patrick Branwell Brontë.* Edited by T. J. Wise and J. A. Symington (Oxford, 1934).

SHEA.   *The Complete Poems of Emily Jane and Anne Brontë.* Edited by T. J. Wise and J. A. Symington (Oxford, 1934).

SHLL.   *The Brontës, Their Lives, Friendship and Correspondence.* Edited by T. J. Wise and J. A. Symington (Oxford, 1932).

The Brontës

Introduction

It may seem a strange paradox that one should be forced at one and the same time to apologize for including the Brontës in a series entitled *Masters of World Literature* and for writing yet another book on the Brontës. The popularity of the Brontës, arising from the easily grasped pathos of their lives, the wide appeal of their novels as simple love stories, and the allurements of both equating and contrasting events in their lives with events in their books, has led to a spate of popular biographies. Such popularity has intimidated critics who have tended to fight shy of biography, who have not seen the love story as a proper literary genre, and who have seen the perils as well as the pleasures of equating fiction with autobiography. The cult of the Brontës can be seen very clearly at their home in Haworth; the thousands of pilgrims who visit this Yorkshire village, hear fragments of oral tradition, see spurious relics, and are exploited by tawdry commercialism, might well imagine that they are visitors to the shrine of some continental saint. Such a cult has not found favour with the high priests of our more austere literary tradition, and just as there are some students of the Brontës who know nothing of any other major literary figure, so there are students of literature who profess to know almost nothing of the Brontës. Emily, it is true, is generally regarded as a novelist of stature, but her slender output and the fact that her genius was not really recognized until long after her death has made it difficult to fit her into any pattern of literary history. Charlotte's reputation has sunk as that of her sister has risen; she has been the victim of the biographical cult, and it is worth remembering that her first novel achieved instant success at a time when nothing was known of her life. Anne's status as a novelist is equally indeterminate; few would deny that she has been rescued from oblivion by the fame of her two sisters, and few would take the heroic step of ignoring her completely.

There would then seem to be room for another attempt to pass judgement on the Brontës. Any such attempt must face the difficulties of steering a middle course between popular acclaim and academic neglect. The perils of the biographical approach are equalled by the perils of ignoring biography altogether. There are dangers in considering the sisters in isolation from one another, as there is plenty of evidence for their close collaboration; and yet it seems equally dangerous to ignore their individuality and the marked differences between them. The presence of a vast corpus of juvenile writings of inferior quality is another hazard; we cannot ignore it completely, but we must not make the mistake of treating these fustian novelettes as true novels. The fact that the juvenilia, the poetry, most of the letters, and even some of the novels of the Brontës have never been properly edited, and that there are problems of texts, dates, and even authorship to be faced is certainly intimidating; amateurs have rushed in where scholars have feared to tread, and in trying to write something new about the Brontës we are faced with a formidable array of old hypotheses masquerading as truths.

After so much abuse of the popular approach to the Brontës it may seem surprising that I acknowledge that this approach is essentially right, and that in *Wuthering Heights, Jane Eyre,* and *Villette* we have three of the greatest English novels. It is this belief, however, which has inspired the following book. Obviously these works receive the most extended treatment; Charlotte's other novels, Anne's novels, and the poems of all three sisters have been given less weight, but I feel they are of interest in themselves as well as being useful guides to the greater novels. The prose juvenilia have been treated with less respect than in most recent studies; but this is partly because problems of authorship must make us reluctant to draw too many conclusions from these stories, and partly because their poor quality must be acknowledged. Unlike the juvenilia the biography of the Brontës is obviously of absorbing interest, but here again a great many uncertainties are involved and most of the rather extended biographical section of this book is devoted to the negative task of showing just how shaky our knowledge of the Brontës' lives is. My main aim in spending so much time on the biography has been to show that the lives of the Brontës are different from their books. The popular cult of the Brontës is right in admiring *Jane Eyre* and right in admiring Charlotte Brontë, but it is wrong in equating the two.

ONE

Biography

The main difficulty in recounting the basic events in the lives of the Brontës is the fact that they have so often been recounted. Patrick Brontë, after making the difficult ascent from Ireland through Cambridge to a curacy in the Church of England, married Maria Branwell in 1812, and the six Brontë children arrived in rapid succession in the following seven years, Maria being born in 1813, Elizabeth in 1815, Charlotte in 1816, Branwell in 1817, Emily in 1818, and Anne in 1820. Three months after the birth of Anne the family moved to Haworth in April 1820, but Mrs. Brontë soon fell ill, dying in September 1821. Her sister, Miss Elizabeth Branwell, came to live in the parsonage to look after the children, and remained there for twenty years, Mr. Brontë's efforts to remarry proving fruitless. In 1824 the two eldest girls were sent to the Clergy Daughters' School at Cowan Bridge, and Charlotte and Emily soon followed them. Maria and Elizabeth Brontë fell ill at this school, and returned home to die in 1825; Charlotte and Emily were thereupon removed from the school, and for the next five years the four remaining children were at home. It was in these years that they embarked upon their precocious career as juvenile authors.

In 1831, Charlotte Brontë was sent to school at Roe Head under Miss Wooler, where she made two firm friends, Ellen Nussey and Mary Taylor. She came home in 1832, but in 1835 returned to Roe Head as a teacher. She was originally accompanied by Emily as a pupil, but within three months Emily was replaced by Anne. At about the same time Branwell made an abortive attempt to enter the Royal Academy in London to study painting. Anne was at Miss Wooler's school until 1837 when she became ill, but Charlotte remained rather unhappily until 1838. Emily also made an attempt, difficult to date exactly,[1] to become a teacher at Law Hill near Halifax, and Branwell tried to become a portrait painter in Bradford. In 1838, all four children were home again, and in 1839, Charlotte received but turned down two offers of marriage, from Henry Nussey, the brother of Ellen, and from Mr. Bryce, a young Irish curate. In the spring of 1839, Anne and Charlotte left home to become governesses at the homes of the Inghams of Blake Hall and Sidgwicks of Stonegappe respectively, Charlotte staying three months and Anne nine. In January 1840, Branwell became tutor to the children of Mr. Postlethwaite of Broughton in Furness, but the girls remained at home, their lives brightened by the presence in Haworth of a new curate, the Rev. William Weightman. In March 1840, Branwell was dismissed by Mr. Postlethwaite, and in October found a job as a clerk on the railways. In 1841, Charlotte took up work briefly with the Whites of Rawdon, and Anne by 1841[2] had found employment with the Robinsons of Thorp Green, but in this year the whole family was much occupied with the thought of the sisters setting up a school of their own. To this end it was decided that Emily and Charlotte should extend their knowledge of French and German on the continent. Anne remained at Thorp Green, and Branwell continued to work as a railway clerk.

Emily and Charlotte left for the school of Madame Heger in Brussels in February 1842, and stayed until November. Their year in Brussels was marred by the dismissal in March of Branwell from his post for negligence, and by the deaths in quick succession of William Weightman, their friend, Martha Taylor, sister of Mary, and finally of their aunt. As a result of this last death Emily and Charlotte returned home, but Charlotte was encouraged to go back to Belgium, more as a teacher than as a pupil, in January 1843, and remained there until the end of the year, suffering considerably from loneliness. Branwell joined Anne at Thorp Green in 1843. The year 1844 was filled with projects for founding a school, but these came to nothing. In this year and the next Charlotte wrote several letters to Monsieur Heger.

In the summer of 1845, Anne and Branwell left the Robinsons,

Branwell being dismissed for grave misconduct, and after this year all four children remained at home. Branwell gave himself up to drink and despair, although he did manage to write some rather desperate poetry and fiction during this period, while his three sisters, who had not ceased to write during their years of employment, now began writing even more seriously. In the autumn of 1845, Charlotte discovered some poems of Emily's, and overcame her reluctance to publish. A selection of poems by the three sisters, writing under the pseudonyms Acton, Currer, and Ellis Bell, was published by Aylott and Jones in May 1846; the terms of publication were hardly advantageous to the sisters. Before this date the three sisters had started looking for someone to publish three works of fiction, presumably *The Professor, Wuthering Heights,* and *Agnes Grey.* In August 1846, Mr. Brontë endured an operation for cataract, and Charlotte began writing *Jane Eyre.*[3] Meanwhile the first three novels continued to go the rounds of various publishers, until eventually the firm of Thomas Newby accepted *Wuthering Heights* and *Agnes Grey,* while Smith, Elder and Co. in rejecting *The Professor* indicated that it would like a three-volume novel from the same author. *Jane Eyre* was sent, immediately accepted, published on October 16th, 1847, and received wide acclamation. *Wuthering Heights* and *Agnes Grey* were published by Newby before the end of the year, and in June 1848 a second novel by Anne, *The Tenant of Wildfell Hall,* appeared in print. Though Newby had not offered favourable terms to Emily and Anne, he had not hesitated to cash in on Charlotte's success by advertising the novels of Emily and Anne as being written by the author of *Jane Eyre.* In July, Anne and Charlotte travelled to London to persuade George Smith of Smith, Elder and Co. that Acton and Currer Bell were separate persons. *The Tenant of Wildfell Hall,* though it received more critical attention than *Agnes Grey,* was attacked, as were *Wuthering Heights* and *Jane Eyre,* for its moral coarseness.

In September 1848, Branwell Brontë died, and Emily rapidly declined in the next two months, dying herself on November 19th. Anne was ill throughout the winter, but survived to make a brief visit to Scarborough, where she died on May 28th, 1849. Charlotte, who had begun *Shirley* while her sisters were still alive, finished it by the end of August, and it was published on October

26th, 1849. By this time Charlotte's identity had become widely known, and it was as the authoress of *Jane Eyre* and *Shirley* that she made in the remaining years of her life a few forays into the literary world. These provided some relief from the loneliness of her life at home, but the writing of her next book, *Villette*, completed in November 1852, took longer than its predecessors. Charlotte was handicapped by ill health and by the distraction in April 1851 of a third proposal of marriage from James Taylor, of Smith, Elder and Co., who left shortly afterwards for India. *Villette* was published on January 28th, 1853, but before this date in December 1852, Charlotte had received a fourth proposal from Arthur Bell Nicholls, her father's curate. The offer was originally refused by Charlotte, and in any case Mr. Brontë was violently opposed to such a marriage, but gradually Mr. Nicholls in spite of leaving his post at Haworth won his way, and in April 1854, Charlotte could write to her friend Ellen Nussey that she was engaged. The marriage took place on June 29th, 1854, and after a honeymoon in Ireland the married couple returned to Haworth. Charlotte began another story, *Emma*, but fell ill in the winter and died on March 31st, 1855.

Such are the bare facts of the Brontës' lives, attested by solid documentary evidence which there is no reason to doubt. Before passing on to the less certain but more exciting area of legend, inference, conjecture, and hypothesis it might be as well to consider the Brontë story as it stands without any adornments. It is not, in spite of the early deaths, unrequited loves, and note of genteel poverty, an especially unhappy story by Victorian standards. Any churchyard bears ample testimony to early mortality as a fact of Victorian life, as common as the early deaths in Victorian fiction would suggest; there is no evidence in the letters of the Brontës of anything like the humiliation that Dickens and Trollope suffered as a result of poverty; the domestic unhappiness of Thackeray or Rossetti should make us cautious in assuming that the Brontës were born under an exceptionally unhappy star. Mrs. Gaskell, the first biographer of the Brontës, herself relatively free, the death of her infant son apart, from her share of Victorian tribulations, is perhaps mainly responsible for the association of the Brontës with high tragedy, but few of her successors in writing about the Brontës have been willing to abandon the tragic note.

And yet Mrs. Gaskell does, perhaps more conspicuously in her letters than in her biography of Charlotte Brontë, strike another note when she comments upon the extraordinary gap between the pathetic, stunted, lonely, and uneventful lives of the Brontës and the richness of their achievement.[4] It could be argued indeed that the extraordinary thing about the Brontës when compared with other writers is that they led lives of such humdrum ordinariness and that the one remarkable event in their story is the publication of their novels, an event which, one might have thought, did much to compensate for earlier unhappiness.

It is perhaps partly the failure of the Brontës to live up to the standard set by some other Victorian writers in leading lives marked by tragedy, misery, and scandal that has led to Brontë biographers laying stress on the more sensational parts of the Brontë story. But a much more important factor leading to sensationalism has of course been the Brontë novels. Biographers, even if they are not novelists, as so many Brontë biographers have been, are by temperament addicted to weaving facts into an interesting story, and when a novelist's biography is being considered, it is very tempting to think that the novelist, too, has woven the facts of his life into an interesting story. Hence the fatal habit has arisen of considering the lives of the Brontës as another Brontë novel, and filling in the uneventful account of their history with the more exciting pages of their fiction.

The controversy over the Clergy Daughters' School at Cowan Bridge is a typical Brontë crux, containing as it does a fair amount of acrimony and conflicting statements, unchecked guesswork, and blurring of fact and fiction.[5] Both Mr. Nicholls and Mrs. Gaskell said that Charlotte had told them that the picture of Lowood in *Jane Eyre* was an accurate portrait of Cowan Bridge, and Charlotte herself in letters to W. S. Williams and Miss Wooler says the same thing, adding rather surprisingly in the latter case that she never thought that Lowood would be recognised. Presumably Charlotte thought she had disguised some parts of her story: after all, unlike Jane Eyre who was sent to the school alone as an orphan in disgrace by her cruel aunt, Charlotte was sent by her father in the company of her sisters, without, one assumes, any stain on her character. But the evidence shows that Charlotte did believe that some parts of her account were true, and what we have to find out is which parts Charlotte thought were true, whether she was right, and how much the equation of Cowan Bridge matters to our appreciation of *Jane Eyre*.

Unfortunately there is not a great deal of trustworthy evidence to help us decide these points. We do have the published works of Carus Wilson, the director of Cowan Bridge School, and these help us to confirm that Carus Wilson was, like Mr. Brocklehurst, a preacher of frightening doctrines obsessed with the salvation of the young, and more interested in the soul than the body. They do not prove him to be, like Mr. Brocklehurst, a hypocrite telling his pupils to avoid vanity and affectation, while his family were guilty of the same sins, nor do they prove him guilty of culpable negligence of his pupils' physical welfare, nor, as Mr. Brocklehurst is to Jane, cruel and unjust.

We have what purports to be a prospectus of Cowan Bridge, with various members of the Wilson family appointed to the staff, and one office held by a scourgemistress, but such a prospectus, though it might seem to prove Mr. Wilson cruel and hypocritical, can hardly be accepted as genuine. We have the registers of the school, showing a number of withdrawals, but even the defenders of Carus Wilson acknowledged that the school had suffered from an infectious disease. We also have various statements made in the controversy over the publication of the first edition of Mrs. Gaskell's life of Charlotte Brontë, but not a great deal of weight can be attached to this testimony, which is often contradictory and confused about dates. We cannot really expect people to be wholly accurate in their memories of what had happened to them at school over thirty years ago; by the same account Charlotte, who was only at the school for a short time when she was very young, cannot be relied upon to give a wholly correct or wholly balanced picture after twenty years.

A slightly more reliable witness would seem to be the superintendent of the school in Charlotte's day, commonly supposed to be portrayed in *Jane Eyre* as Miss Temple. As an adult, portrayed in fiction as a just woman, with no motive for finding fault with Charlotte Brontë, who had praised her so highly, "Miss Temple" might seem to be a valuable advocate for the side of Carus Wilson, and certainly her praise of his school, quoted in the third edition of Mrs. Gaskell's life, did much to remove the bitter impression

left by the first edition. Unfortunately there seems a strange confusion about the identity of "Miss Temple,"[6] and her testimony,
delivered at second hand, is perhaps not all that impressive. All
that the real Miss Temple's husband is alleged to have said in a
letter to one of Mr. Wilson's friends is: "Often have I heard my
late wife speak of her sojourn at Cowan Bridge; always in terms
of admiration of Mr. Carus Wilson, his parental love to his pupils,
and their love for him; of the food and general treatment, in terms
of approval. I have heard her allude to an unfortunate cook, who
used at times to spoil the porridge, but who, she said, was soon
dismissed" (G., p. 75).

The case against Cowan Bridge and Carus Wilson is not really
proven, nor perhaps is it worth proving. For the sake of our appreciation of *Jane Eyre* it is probably best if we assume that Lowood
is neither an exact reproduction of Cowan Bridge nor a complete
figment of Charlotte's imagination. If we took the latter view we
would lose our faith in Charlotte's veracity as a reporter, but if
we took the view of most Brontë biographers and simply equated
Lowood with Cowan Bridge, we might lose our faith in the artistic
integrity of *Jane Eyre*. For if Charlotte had simply copied out a
section from her life at the beginning of her novel, we would find
it hard to see the relevance of the Lowood section to the rest of it.
It is justifiable to trace parallels between St. John Rivers and Mr.
Brocklehurst, but we cannot do this if we think of Mr. Brocklehurst as Carus Wilson. It is possible to say that the path of stoic
resignation adopted by Helen Burns and to a lesser extent by Miss
Temple is not presented as wholly admirable in the novel, but
we cannot do this if we regard Helen Burns as Maria Brontë or
Miss Temple as Miss Evans, although the eventual defence by
Miss Evans of Carus Wilson does perhaps draw attention to the
slightly equivocal position of her fictional equivalent in *Jane Eyre*.

The Brontës were only at Cowan Bridge for a short time, but
lived with their father for most of their lives. It might therefore
seem important to establish whether the charges of eccentricity,
selfishness, snobbery, male chauvinism, and negligence that have
been levelled at Mr. Brontë at various times and at various times
vigorously rebuffed are true or not.[7] As with Cowan Bridge we
have the usual pattern of stories from one source that are flatly
contradicted by someone else, such as Mrs. Gaskell's account,

denied by Mr. Brontë, of his tearing up his wife's dress, and several incidents where the evidence is not complete: we can hardly accuse Mr. Brontë of culpable negligence in letting his children stay at Cowan Bridge until we know for certain that Cowan Bridge was a bad school. The accusation that Mr. Brontë neglected his daughters in favour of his son with dire results for both parties is one easily made in modern times, but Victorians would hardly have found such conduct reprehensible. On the other hand both Mary Taylor and Mrs. Gaskell condemned Mr. Brontë, and the charges of selfishness, snobbery, and eccentricity do seem to be supported by Mr. Brontë's own correspondence and notes in his books, which do seem to show a rather morbid preoccupation with his own welfare.

What is lacking is any evidence for the three Brontë sisters blaming their father in any way. Nor can we use the Brontës' novels to provide evidence for filial feeling or the lack of it because Brontë heroines and heroes are singularly short of fathers. In the novels of Anne and Charlotte, Agnes Grey is the only heroine or hero whose father is alive when the novel opens, and he dies fairly rapidly. Oddly enough it is Emily Brontë, usually thought to be the sister who drew least upon her experience and most upon her imagination, who in *Wuthering Heights* paints some quite full portraits of normal and abnormal relationships between fathers and children, although even here the relationships are terminated by early deaths. The absence of fathers in the Brontë novels could be interpreted in various ways. We could say that the Brontës were so deprived of their father's companionship that they felt themselves orphaned of both parents, or we could say that the tie between father and daughter was such a close and sacred one that they dare not touch upon it in their fiction. In the absence of any evidence we cannot assume either interpretation, but must simply note that in this case there is a very large gap between the lives of the Brontës and their books.

The Brontës' aunt died before they had embarked upon their career as novelists, but Brontë biographers have not hesitated to ascribe a large and sinister influence to her.[8] Jane Eyre's aunt is cruel, Helen Huntingdon's aunt in trying to dissuade, quite rightly as it turns out, Helen from marrying Arthur preaches orthodox doctrines of eternal punishment, and Caroline Helstone's possessed some mad Methodist magazines. On this extremely slender basis it has all too readily been assumed that the Brontës' early lives were darkened by their aunt's dire influence. It has even been assumed that the Calvinistic worries about preordination to damnation which troubled Anne, Charlotte, and Branwell at various stages in their lives were a result of their aunt's teaching, although here unless we confuse Calvinism with Methodism or belief in predestination with belief in eternal punishment there is no evidence even in the Brontës' novels for supposing any Calvinistic influence from an aunt. In the Brontës' letters there is no indication that Miss Branwell was at all sinister: what information we have suggests the opposite.

A much more potent influence, at any rate for Charlotte, was Monsieur Heger. Here at last we do seem on solid ground in suggesting a link between the life of Charlotte and her books. Monsieur Heger was a married Belgian schoolmaster; Mr. Rochester is married, Robert Moore is half Belgian, Louis Moore half Belgian and a schoolmaster, Edward Crimsworth a schoolmaster who teaches in Belgium, and Paul Emanuel a Belgian schoolmaster whose marriage to Lucy Snowe is opposed by a Belgian schoolmistress looking very like Madame Heger. The obvious inference that Charlotte was in love with Monsieur Heger was made by students of the novels, but loyally denied by Brontë biographers until the discovery in 1913 of four letters written by Charlotte to Monsieur Heger, suggesting some degree of passionate attachment on Charlotte's part.[9]

So far so good, but we cannot immediately start rewriting the story of Charlotte's stay in Belgium from the pages of *Villette*. There is one very important difference between Monsieur Heger and Paul Emanuel, and that is that Monsieur Heger was married. Unlike Mr. Rochester's wife, his wife was not mad, but a successful schoolmistress enjoying, as far as one can see, a happy married life. When Jane Eyre finds that Mr. Rochester is married, although many would feel with Mr. Rochester that such a marriage hardly counted, Jane Eyre feels that it does matter, and takes the drastic step of leaving him. What then were Charlotte's feelings when she discovered that she was in love with a married man? When did she discover them? How aware were her sisters of her situation?

How far did Monsieur Heger encourage her and how much did Madame Heger discourage her?

These are questions that are easy to ask, but impossible to answer from the evidence of Charlotte's novels, because Charlotte did not write a novel about someone in her position. She does make a few cryptic references to her unhappiness in letters to other correspondents, and we do have her letters to Monsieur Heger, but even these are unsatisfactory. Quite apart from the peculiar story of the preservation of these letters, torn up by Monsieur Heger, but stuck together by his wife, it is clear from internal and external evidence that there were more letters than the four that have been preserved,[10] and to establish the exact truth about the affair we would also like to have any letters written by Monsieur Heger to Charlotte. In the absence of any further evidence we can only speculate on what happened in Charlotte's life and note that it is different from what happened in Charlotte's novels.

A parallel love affair for Anne Brontë has also been postulated.[11] Like Charlotte she wrote unhappy love poetry, and like Charlotte she wrote a novel in which a heroine, like herself a governess, falls in love with a man who is superficially like a character in the Brontës' lives. Just as the Brontës only knew well one married Belgian schoolmaster, so too they only knew one pleasant young curate, and so the equation of Mr. Weston in *Agnes Grey* with Mr. Weightman in real life has been assumed. The equation is easy to make, less easy to justify. We have no support from the Brontës' letters for any love affair for Anne. The evidence of the poems is unimpressive, since Emily too wrote love poetry without falling in love, though we should perhaps pay some attention to the fact that Anne did not publish poems which might seem to refer to Mr. Weightman. As the least successful writer of the three sisters, Anne is often supposed to be the most limited in her experience of the world, being thus driven back to autobiography; in fact, though the least successful writer, Anne was the most successful governess, and in her years at Thorp Green she may have read about, heard about or even met characters more like Mr. Weston than Mr. Weightman.

Since only *Agnes Grey* is really affected by Mr. Weightman, it is perhaps not a very important controversy. A more crucial difficulty arises when we consider the possible love affair between Branwell Brontë and his employer's wife, Lydia Robinson.[12] Branwell had of course shown himself in an unsatisfactory light on previous occasions, but his return home in disgrace in 1845 is more important both because it was so final and because it occurred just at the beginning of his sisters' careers as novelists. The achievement of the Brontë sisters in writing at a time when their brother was such a source of misery has often been stressed, but the contribution of Branwell to novels full of violence, drunkenness, and marital infidelity has been insufficiently stated, and it is because Branwell would seem to be an important influence on *Wuthering Heights*, *The Tenant of Wildfell Hall*, and *Jane Eyre* that we would like to know more about his story.

What we would like to learn is exactly what happened at Thorp Green. It would seem that something disgraceful occurred, since otherwise Branwell would hardly have been dismissed. On his return home Branwell put forward the story that he had fallen in love with Mrs. Robinson, and she with him, and this story, mirrored in Branwell's poetry and fiction, appears to have been believed by the Brontë family, who were naturally inclined to put most of the blame on Mrs. Robinson. As such it appeared in the first edition of Mrs. Gaskell's life, but Mrs. Robinson objected to being described as a vile seducer, and the story had to be dropped in the third edition, although it is still commonly believed.

A contrary theory is that Branwell invented the whole love affair as a cover for some more disgraceful episode, perhaps involving the Robinson boy. It is true that Branwell imagined that Mrs. Robinson was ill with love for him, at the time of her husband's death in June 1846 a year after Branwell's dismissal when we have factual evidence that she was busy with financial arrangements of her husband's estate, and that he believed that Mr. Robinson had prevented his wife marrying Branwell by a codicil in his will when no such codicil existed. It is also true that Branwell was as ready as any Brontë biographer to confuse fact and fiction, and that we cannot use his fictional writings as evidence of what happened at Thorp Green. There is nothing in the Robinson papers to suggest any breach between Mr. Robinson and his wife, and indeed some evidence to suggest affection between them at the time of Branwell's dismissal, though we must remember Victorian readiness to cover up old scandals: Mr. Robinson would not be the first husband to forgive his wife but punish her partner in adultery.

On the other hand it is difficult to suggest any other scandal sufficiently grave both for Branwell to be dismissed and for Branwell to invent the story of falling in love with Mrs. Robinson as an excuse. Drunkenness is less romantic than adultery, and Mr. Robinson could well dismiss Branwell for being in charge of his son when drunk or perhaps for encouraging him to drink, but would Branwell really have invented a romantic excuse to cover a squalid sin, if his family would have thought the romantic excuse more heinous than the squalid truth? The language of both Mr. Robinson in dismissing Branwell for conduct too disgraceful to mention and of Anne Brontë, who said that she had had at Thorp Green some very unpleasant and undreamt-of experiences of human nature, suggests some crime worse than drunkenness. A homosexual relationship with Edmund Robinson has been suggested, but, although we must make allowances for Victorian skill in concealing that particular skeleton, it remains true that there is no evidence for this suggestion beyond the fact that Edmund Robinson died unmarried.

At this stage we can perhaps use the Brontë novels as evidence, if not for what had happened at Thorp Green, at any rate for what the Brontës thought had happened. *Wuthering Heights*, *Jane Eyre*, and *The Tenant of Wildfell Hall* were all thought shocking when they appeared, and for us reared on *Madame Bovary* and *Anna Karenina*, where adultery is treated sympathetically, and modern novels, where it is taken for granted, it is very hard to see what all the fuss was about. Jane Eyre and Helen Huntingdon indignantly shrink away from any suggestion that they should commit adultery, Arthur Huntingdon's affair with Lady Lowborough is treated with horror, and even Heathcliff's affair with Catherine, where the question of adultery is hardly raised, meets with sufficient indignation from Nelly Dean to silence any critics. But critics would not be silenced, because in the climate in which the Brontës were writing it was not sufficient to speak of adultery with disapproval: the subject should not be mentioned at all.

It is therefore tempting to ascribe to Branwell's affair with Mrs. Robinson the Brontës' willingness to break with Victorian convention. We cannot do this with complete confidence because even before Branwell had gone to Thorp Green, Charlotte and Emily were writing in their juvenilia about heroes and heroines who paid little attention to the formalities of the marriage tie. What is significant here is that such heroes and heroines are not treated with any disapproval, and a good case might be made out for saying that it was Branwell's affair with Mrs. Robinson which enabled the Brontës to see the reality behind the romantic postures of Angria and Gondal.

Branwell's escapades are more exciting than the dreary record of his sisters as teachers and governesses, and have consequently received more attention from biographers.[13] And yet the position of a teacher is important in most of the novels. It is tempting to supplement our scanty knowledge of the Brontës' careers as governesses from the pages of *Agnes Grey* and *Jane Eyre*, and our account of Charlotte's life as a schoolteacher from *The Professor* and *Villette*. It is true that some of the attitudes displayed by the protagonists of these books were shown by the Brontës themselves; we know from the Brontës' letters that they disliked the subservient role of governess, despised the intellectual inferiority of their employers, did not like spoilt children, and pined for the independence achieved by the headmistress of a school; it is not surprising that these themes recur throughout the novels. It is therefore tempting to make a parallel equation between events in the careers of Brontë heroines and events in the lives of their creators; but this temptation should be resisted. Like Agnes Grey, Anne Brontë had two employers, but there is some evidence to show that the Inghams of Blake Hall were not particularly similar to the vulgar Bloomfields, more like Charlotte's employers, the Whites of Rawdon, and there are also differences, especially in matters of religion, between the Robinsons and the Murrays. In *Agnes Grey* the heroine cannot really cope with the ill-behaved Bloomfield children, but makes a qualified success in her post as governess with the Murrays, and judging from the length of her stay with the Inghams and Robinsons and references to friendly visits from the Robinson girls after Anne had left, there may be a correspondence between fact and fiction here. Charlotte's career as a governess was much shorter than Anne's, and there seems nothing in what we know of her stay with the Sidgwicks or Whites that resembles Jane Eyre's successful teaching of Adèle Varens or her life in the village school at Morton. The rancour expressed by Jane Eyre against Blanche Ingram, and the speeches about her employers, the Hardmans, put into the mouth of Caroline Helstone's mother, may reflect Charlotte's indignation against the way governesses were treated generally, but we would be mistaken in thinking that the Sidgwicks and Whites were anything like as aristocratic as the Ingrams and Hardmans are meant to be.

It has generally been assumed that the school scenes in *The Professor* and *Villette* are taken from real life. Since the Belgian scenery seems fairly authentic, certain other incidents such as the visit to the confessional are autobiographical, and certain scenes in *The Professor* are repeated in *Villette*, this assumption does not seem unreasonable. On the other hand we must also remember the strong element of wishful thinking in the educational sphere that pervades both novels; both novels depict successful teachers who are eventually rewarded by having a school of their own. We know Charlotte wanted to have a school of her own, and presumably she wanted to be a successful teacher, but this does not mean that she *was* a successful teacher. The evidence from her former pupils is hardly conclusive: Charlotte's lack of success as a governess, her morbidity and her loneliness would suggest that she hardly equalled either Edward Crimsworth or Lucy Snowe. On the other hand, and here the dangers of taking the novels as autobiographical can be demonstrated, there is no evidence that she was as unsuccessful as Frances Henri.

It is of course possible that Charlotte may be drawing upon the experience of Emily in her portrait of Frances Henri. This raises the question of how much the sisters collaborated in writing their novels. We have in this case what appears to be a clear statement by Charlotte to Mrs. Gaskell[14] to the effect that the sisters used to read to one another what they had written, but that this rarely caused Charlotte to alter what she had written; we also have the whole tradition of joint authorship in the juvenilia. On the other hand Emily's indignation at the discovery of her poetry, and the existence of two separate cycles of Gondal and Angria, would seem to argue against close collaboration at certain stages in the Brontës' writing careers, at any rate between Charlotte and her sisters. There is internal as well as external evidence for Emily and Anne working closely together during the writing of *The Tenant of Wildfell Hall* and *Wuthering Heights*, but we can be less confident about assuming the same degree of collaboration where other novels are concerned;[15] the other novels are assumed to be more embarrassingly autobiographical, and this is perhaps another reason why the sisters might be less willing to share their work.

Branwell's share in his sisters' work is another problem. Close contact with Charlotte during the writing of the juvenilia is established.[16] It is still not yet established how much of what is commonly accepted as being written by Charlotte was in fact written by Branwell and ascribed to Charlotte in order to render it more valuable as a collector's item. The rough masculine tone of some of these suspect juvenile writings might seem an argument in favour of Branwell's authorship, but the same argument might be used in deciding the authorship of *Wuthering Heights*. Three of Branwell's acquaintances claimed that he had some part in *Wuthering Heights*, though his family denied this. His family's acceptance of Emily's authorship might seem conclusive, were it not for the fact that so much about Emily and Branwell is doubtful and disputed. His family believed Branwell to have been seduced by Mrs. Robinson, and only one of his acquaintances thought Branwell had invented the whole story; yet it is considered quite respectable to believe Leyland and disbelieve the Brontë family when discussing the Robinson affair, although it is not respectable to believe Dearden, George Searle Phillips, and Grundy when deciding the authorship of *Wuthering Heights*.[17]

It is probably thought disrespectful to question the authorship of *Wuthering Heights*, because through the greatness of *Wuthering Heights*, which few would deny, the fame of Emily Brontë has grown to such an extent that it seems almost irreverent to speak of her work and her life except in hushed superlatives. Few have had the courage to admit that though much of her poetry is interesting and some poems outstanding, there are sections of her verse which barely rise above the dreary clichés of the Angrian prose narratives. Thus one argument against Branwell's authorship falls to the ground: if Emily, and for that matter, Charlotte too, could produce a work of genius after writing so badly, so could Branwell, usually acknowledged to be the second-best poet of the family. It does seem improbable that Emily, in spite of her reluctance to publish her poems and her strange silence after the writing of *Wuthering Heights*, should really have imposed a lie upon her sisters, and perhaps the spectre of Branwell as the author of *Wuthering Heights* had better be relegated to the limbo of unproved and unprovable Brontë conjectures.

We can, however, raise a few questions about the personality of Emily. Charlotte's praise of her after her death obviously affected Mrs. Gaskell deeply, and all subsequent biographers have followed Charlotte and her biographer in making the author of "No Coward Soul is Mine" and *Wuthering Heights* fit her own writings. Charlotte compared her to Shirley Keeldar; and it is a character combining Shirley's brilliance with Heathcliff's power that stalks through many a Brontë biography. There is not a great deal of evidence to support this impressive portrait. There is the record of a few courageous escapades involving dogs, support of Branwell during his decline, the story of his rescue from fire, and Emily's own heroic death, the details of which are not fully authenticated. Against this we have to balance Emily's homesickness, her repeated inability to survive for long as a pupil or a teacher, the homely triviality of her surviving letters and diary papers. The rapidity with which Emily Brontë died could be emphasised as much as the more commonly vaunted refusal to admit that she was ill. In one of her few fairly well authenticated remarks attested by Ellen Nussey in *Scribner's Monthly*,[18] Emily is said to be concerned with the battle between the weak and the strong, and there would seem to be the same enigmatic blend of weakness and strength in *Wuthering Heights* and in her own life.

We might be able to speak of Emily Brontë with a little more confidence if we knew whether she had written a second novel, but this is one final Brontë problem, where the evidence is fairly evenly balanced.[19] On the one hand we have a letter from Newby about a new novel, found next to and fitting an envelope addressed to Ellis Bell, and placed, presumably by Charlotte, in Emily's writing desk. In addition we have the almost complete absence of anything in prose or poetry written by Emily after *Wuthering Heights*. On the other hand we would expect Charlotte or Mrs. Gaskell to have made some definite reference to another novel, and since Newby on other occasions confused Acton and Ellis Bell, he could be merely referring to Anne's second novel, *The Tenant of Wildfell Hall*.

All these problems are annoying, because so much labour has been spent in trying to solve them, so much of it wasted, engendering confusion rather than clearing it up, and it would seem that so little extra evidence was required to clear them up finally. We can console ourselves with the reflection that if we were to solve them by the sudden discovery of new Brontëana, our knowledge and appreciation of the Brontë novels would not be greatly enhanced. Let us suppose that we found irrefutable independent testimony that Cowan Bridge was not accurately portrayed in Lowood, that Mr. Brontë was selfish, and Miss Branwell kind. Let us add to this some compromising letters from Mrs. Robinson to Branwell, some more innocently compromising letters from Charlotte to Monsieur Heger and Anne to Mr. Weightman, and a full and unbiased account of the Brontës as teachers and governesses from someone who knew them in these capacities. Finally let us add some information about Emily, a statement or two from her after 1845, a few pages from another novel, and an account of the extent to which she had shared and discussed her work with her sisters. Such discoveries might seem impossible at this late stage, but after the discovery of the Heger letters and the juvenilia, few would be willing to state categorically that no new Brontë evidence will ever materialize. In view of the atmosphere of controversy, secrecy, inefficiency, and dishonesty that has surrounded the lives of the Brontës, it seems more than likely that there is still some material waiting to make the name of some fortunate scholar. But would the discovery of any or all of this information really further our interpretation and assessment of the Brontës' novels? An analysis of the novels suggests that biographical enquiries have been up to now an obstacle to proper criticism; more accurate biographical information might only make the obstacle more formidable.

TWO

Juvenilia

Students of the Brontës can argue whether the biography of the sisters has proved more of an obstacle than a guide to the interpretation of their novels, and much the same can be said of the Brontë juvenilia. Few, however, have dared to make the latter point. The discovery by Miss F. E. Ratchford that most of the poetry and prose written by the Brontës before the publication of the novels was not a series of disconnected fragments but parts of two enormous cycles of stories came at a time when there was a reaction against biographical and psychological studies, and Miss Ratchford's researches were eagerly seized upon as providing a different kind of clue to the Brontës. The inaccessibility of the widely scattered manuscripts has meant we have to rely for information about them upon those who, like Miss Ratchford, have published them; and those who have edited Brontë juvenilia are normally inclined to stress their literary value.[1] The tiny manuscripts in their print-like script have a romantic and pathetic air about them, and this has perhaps blinded students into a false assessment of their worth. The juvenilia do have a certain biographical interest, and we should perhaps consider them first for the light they shed on the Brontë story.

In June 1826, as Branwell later recorded, Mr. Brontë brought back twelve wooden soldiers; the Brontë children, of whom the eldest, Charlotte, was ten, began inventing stories about them; and by 1829 they had started committing these stories to writing. These early tales, strongly influenced by what the children had read in *Blackwood's Magazine*, were mainly concerned with the establishment by European heroes, roughly based on the twelve soldiers, of an imaginary kingdom in West Africa. Originally Charlotte's chief hero was the Duke of Wellington, while Branwell showed interest in Marshal Soult, a chivalrous French general in the Peninsular Wars. After describing the founding of the city of Glass Town, later known as Verdopolis, Charlotte became more interested in the Duke of Wellington's son, Arthur Adrian Welles-ley, while Branwell's principal character was appropriately named Alexander Rogue. Rogue, also known as Percy, and subsequently ennobled as Lord Ellrington and Earl of Northangerland, and Wellesley, also known as the Marquess of Douro and the Duke of Zamorna, are the two chief characters in the stories written by Charlotte and Branwell. After 1833 most of these are set in a realm known as Angria, lying to the east of Verdopolis. Zamorna, after a previous marriage to Marian Hume, is married to North-angerland's daughter, Mary Percy, but neither of the two chief heroes has much respect for the marriage tie. On the whole, if the attributions to each are to be believed, Charlotte was more con-cerned with the love affairs of the two heroes, while Branwell was occupied with war and politics.

Before 1834, Emily and Anne Brontë, who because of their age do not seem to have played much part in the earlier stories, had broken away and set up their own cycle concerning an island in the Pacific known as Gondal. We know this from the first of four diary papers which Emily and Anne wrote at roughly four-yearly intervals until 1845, and it is clear from the evidence of these diary papers that for most of their writing lives Anne and Emily were occupied with Gondal, although none of the prose concerned with Gondal has survived. Charlotte and Branwell were less faith-ful to Angria; their separation from each other, discouraging advice from the poet laureate Southey to Charlotte, a feeling well expressed in her diary written at Roe Head that it was wrong to give way to the imagination, and a greater desire for realism, which shows itself in some of the later stories, all led to the abandonment of Angria. In about 1839, Charlotte finally bade farewell to the burning clime of Angria, and there are no more Angrian stories written by her after this date, although there are one or two fragments, very reminiscent of *The Professor*, in which characters from Angria appear in a Yorkshire setting.[2] Charlotte was not inactive as a writer between 1839 and 1845, but did not preserve what she had written. Branwell, whose first major lapse occurred in 1840, when he was dismissed from his position at Mr. Postlethwaite's, does not appear to have written a great deal after this date; he was becoming increasingly alienated from Charlotte, although there are a few stories, which like Charlotte's are a mixture of Angrian romance and Yorkshire realism. There is a good case for regarding 1840 as providing a dividing line between the Brontë juvenilia and their mature writings.[3]

This being so, we can consider whether the Brontës' writing in the ten years or so before 1840 is really as impressive or extraordinary as has been generally maintained. In our own age, dominated by a variety of forms of amusement, we tend to forget how common writing as a means of entertainment was in the Victorian age. It was particularly noticeable in families where more than one member had literary tastes; we can compare the Arnold and Rossetti families here. A less strenuous form of entertainment was reading, but here the Brontës through poverty and isolation were handicapped. We cannot, therefore, be surprised that the Brontës wrote when young; though their enormous output, equal, it has been calculated, to their published works, is perhaps surprising. What is remarkable about the Brontës' juvenilia in view of their later eminence is that so much of what they wrote is so bad.

This may seem a harsh statement, ignoring as it does the extreme youth of the Brontës when they first began writing, the fact that they were not writing for publication, and the inadequate editing which has inevitably resulted in many of the stories lacking any sort of coherence. Nevertheless an examination of five of the latest juvenile stories, recently edited with lavish care by Miss Winifred Gérin, suggests that the writing of the Brontës in the 1830s left a great deal of room for improvement.

It is difficult to give an adequate summary of these five tales because they are so incoherent. Of course the whole nature of the Angrian cycle is such that the closed circle of those acquainted with Angrian politics and personalities can readily understand references to events which baffle the general reader new to the juvenilia. The statement is sometimes made that both the Angrian and Gondal cycles are epics; while unfair to great epics like the *Iliad* and the *Odyssey*, it does draw attention to a feature which the Brontës' juvenile writing shares with heroic poetry orally composed, namely, the ability of the composer of the cycle to draw on a stock of common knowledge and introduce characters and references without a great deal of background and explanation. Even when we have made allowance for this, we are still left baffled by the confusion of these juvenile novelettes with their constant shifts of focus, gaps in narrative, unhelpful introductions, and unresolved conclusions.

The title of the first work in Miss Gérin's collection, *Passing Events*, hardly suggests organic unity, and there is a revealing passage early on in the work where the author confesses:

> I would fain fall into some regular strain of composition, but I cannot, my mind is like a prism full of colours but not of forms. A thousand tints are there, brilliant and varied, and if they would resolve into the shade of some flower or bird or gem, I could picture before you. I feel I could. A Panorama is round me whose scenes shift before I can at all fix their features. (FN., pp. 38–39)

The scenes that follow—a portrait of Northangerland's wife Zenobia, a portrait of Zamorna's mistress Mina Laury, a description of a Methodist service, a brief account of Mary Percy, torn between her loyalty to her father Northangerland and husband Zamorna, and a series of sketches describing the confused state of Angria as it faces the civil war between Northangerland and Zamorna—are varied, but hardly brilliant. A promising source of unity in the first three episodes would seem to be the figure of Louisa Vernon, also known as Louisa Dance and the Countess of Wellesley. She is mentioned in the first episode, appears and confronts Zamorna in the second, and is present at the sermon in the third. But what she is doing on either of these two later occasions is not clear; indeed her reappearance in the third episode is surprising, since the second scene closes with her disappearance and the words "she has not since been heard of."

Julia is another episodic work in which it is even harder to see what is happening or meant to be happening. We first find a picture of rural life near Evesham, then a portrait of a group of rather bored and boring aristocrats centred round Lady Julia Thornton, cousin of Zamorna, then, reverting to the former narrative, a brutally cynical account of a Methodist meeting near

Evesham. The civil war between Northangerland and Zamorna still looms large, and in the middle of it we find again Louisa Vernon, and a new character, her daughter by Northangerland, Caroline. Like most of the female characters in the Angrian cycle, Louisa and Caroline are torn between Northangerland and Zamorna. Perhaps the most noteworthy feature of *Julia* is the contrast between the inflated language of parts of it, and the coarse realism of other episodes. Thus Zamorna's Byronic musings are described in the following way:

Recollection aided the fiend that disturbed him in a mirror of wondrous truth, it showed him her image as he had seen it a hundred times—young, pallid, seldom smiling, waiting his approach in a saloon of gorgeous State—gnawed with Doubt till his step comes surrounded with the morbid visions of love maddened to jealousy—visions that dissolved to rapture, when the closing day at last darkened over him at her side. (FN., p. 113)

We can compare with this the closing words of the extract from the Methodist preacher's journal:

I was scourged, I was dragged through a horse-pond, I was drowned under a deluge from the pump—Nay, I have good reason to believe that more than one pistol was discharged at my head—but I survived all, and by the blessing of God was that night able to make a hearty supper and to sleep as soundly as ever I did in my life. My master avenged me in his own good time, about a fortnight after, I saw the dead body of Rhodes dragged out of his house, and with the rope that he had been hung with still round his neck—I beheld him flung into that very horse-pond where by his orders I had been nearly murdered.[4] (FN., pp. 104–105)

The next three tales are a little easier to analyse, and since they are supposed to be written later than *Julia* and *Passing Events*, they do lend a certain amount of support to the view that in the Angrian tales we can trace Charlotte's gradual improvement as a writer. *Mina Laury* is mainly concerned with the character we have already met in *Passing Events*; like Jane Eyre she has been a governess, unlike Jane Eyre she is the mistress of the irresistible Zamorna, although most of *Mina Laury* is concerned with her indignant rejection of the proposals of Lord Hartford. Most of the emphasis of the novelette is on Mina Laury and her feelings for Zamorna, but towards the end of the work, in an episode apparently borrowed from *Passing Events*, Zamorna's wife arrives in disguise, and the work ends with a reconciliation between her and her husband. This change of focus is disturbing, and yet *Mina Laury* is one of the best of the juvenilia. The greater realism, whereby Zamorna is introduced to us at the breakfast table in his dressing gown, is a sign of improvement.

The next tale, entitled *Captain Henry Hastings*, is much longer, and we find the same disturbing shifts of narrator and gaps in the narrative as in *Julia* and *Passing Events*. Unlike these tales, however, there would seem to be some kind of central theme to the story, and this is the relationship between the dissolute and drunken Henry Hastings and his virtuous and resolute sister Elizabeth. A parallel with Branwell and Charlotte has been drawn by Brontë biographers, especially as Elizabeth Hastings is described both as small and as a teacher, and the passages in which Hastings describes his escapades are considered to be reflections of Branwell's way of talking. One wonders whether by 1839, Branwell was quite so openly dissolute as Hastings, and whether Charlotte really heard Branwell talking like this.

Wilson spoke of his associates, of his pals, a short time before he fell under the table—he drank in a brimming bumper d——mn——n to the Soldan and his satellites. (FN., p. 191)

Zamorna appears in *Captain Henry Hastings* only right at the end, in a scene of reconciliation with his duchess. He is, however, one of the central characters in *Caroline Vernon*, which describes the growing passion of a young girl for the duke. This story contains none of the violent language of *Captain Henry Hastings*, but its sentiments are still surprising from the author of *Jane Eyre*. Mina Laury acknowledges that she is Zamorna's mistress, but seems a little guilty about this, and shows some sense of virtue in resisting the importunities of Lord Hartford. Caroline Vernon, in spite of her greater youth and the fact that Zamorna's wife is her half-sister, feels no guilt. Whereas Mina Laury's surrender to the duke is an accomplished fact of the past, and her subservient role as governess to the duke's children might seem to render her transference to the role of mistress less shocking, Caroline is Zamorna's ward, and a full account of her unwardlike behaviour is given.

There are realistic touches about the tale, as when Zamorna is found in a hayfield, "not exactly in his shirt sleeves" (FN., p. 285), and there is a strange letter from an African character called Quashia full of phrases like a "cab of Dove's dung" (FN., p. 283), but these are at odds with the more Gothic descriptions of Zamorna's predicament.

In *Captain Henry Hastings* a hit over the ear is described as "a manual application on to the auricular organs" (FN., p. 265), and one sometimes wonders whether those who have made claims on behalf of the Brontë juvenilia are not guilty of a similar extravagant pomposity. It is obviously ridiculous to maintain that the juvenilia are great works of art in themselves; any claim for them must rest on the fact that they were supposed to be written by the authors of great novels, and they are worthy of attention only insofar as they shed light on these novels. Various arguments have been put forward to show that they are valuable or even essential for an appreciation of the Brontës' mature work, but these arguments are hardly convincing.

It is first maintained that the juvenilia prove conclusively that Branwell could have had no part in his sister's adult writings. Both Miss Ratchford and Miss Gérin are at pains to contrast Branwell's dreary chronicling of Angrian history with Charlotte's more interesting explorations of Angrian characters. Both admit to a considerable degree of collaboration between Branwell and Charlotte, and it seems surprising that stories allegedly influenced by Branwell should be supposed to prove Charlotte's superiority to Branwell. It also seems hard to prove any kind of superiority from such bad writing. Furthermore, it is not at all clear that some of the stories which are meant to show that Charlotte had the seeds of genius in her were not in fact written by the supposedly pedestrian Branwell.[5] The fact that the Brontë juvenilia passed through the hands of the notoriously disreputable literary forger T. J. Wise must arouse our suspicions, and in fact the five novelettes published by Miss Gérin are in any case suspicious. The incoherent narrative, and the changes of style, would suggest joint authorship. The repeated scenes of drunkenness and the note of brutal cynicism would suggest Branwell's hand. Signatures of Charlotte Brontë or the pseudonym, C. Townshend, are as unconvincing as they are easy to forge. *Caroline Vernon* has no signature, and

Passing Events has a signature in the middle as well as the end. It would be easy to pass off a manuscript as Charlotte's by attaching a small section of a story by her to a larger section by Branwell, and *Captain Henry Hastings*, where Zamorna's entry in Chapter V is unexpected and the note of reconciliation in Chapter VI even more so, might well be such a manuscript.

If Branwell wrote some of the juvenilia commonly attributed to Charlotte we cannot be very confident about drawing biographical conclusions from these juvenilia. *Captain Henry Hastings* might be a reflection of Charlotte's feelings for her brother in the year 1839, although there is no other evidence for Charlotte being so shocked by Branwell's dissipation at so early a date; the story of Henry and Elizabeth Hastings would seem to mirror more accurately Branwell's romantic vision of his plight, as shown in his poetry written at roughly this time. In any case we have shown that it is dangerous to seek biographical facts from works of fiction; if this is true of the novels, it must be even more true of the juvenilia, so much more remote from reality. The only biographical information that the juvenilia do provide is that they show how preoccupied the Brontës were with their romantic dream world in their humdrum existence, but we know this already from Charlotte's Roe Head journal.

Unable to make much of any connections between the characters in the Brontës' lives and characters in the juvenilia, since they are so different, admirers of the juvenilia have turned their attention to tracing parallels between the juvenilia and the novels. Here we do seem on solid ground at last. Zamorna with his high-handed irresistible manner, his mistresses and Byronic gloom is fairly close to Mr. Rochester, especially in the more realistic later stories. It is not clear, however, how much we gain by seeing this rough sketch of Rochester, especially as we know already that the Brontës were interested in the Byronic hero. Other parallels are more strained. Mina Laury is like Jane Eyre in her subservient position and total acceptance of love, but the vital difference between her and Jane is that she is Zamorna's mistress. Attempts to trace the ancestor of Paul Emanuel not in Monsieur Heger, but in Zamorna's happily married prime minister Warner, of Mrs. Rochester in Northangerland's wife, and of Rochester's ward

Adèle Varens in Caroline Vernon are obviously absurd, nor is the point of such absurdities at all clear.[6]

Nor is it clear how an examination of the style of the juvenilia is instructive in preparing us for the mature novels. If we are looking for faults in the novels, such as uncertainty of narrative focus, wavering between realism and romance, a temptation to indulge in scenes of high life with insufficient knowledge, and a tendency to pompous circumlocutions, we can find these in abundance in the juvenilia; but it does no service to the mature novels to start looking for faults in this way, and we can only marvel that Charlotte Brontë corrected these faults so rapidly. If we are looking for the first sign of the mature novels' merits in the juvenilia, our task is harder; there is the capacity to explore feeling but not to express it in the juvenilia, and the recognition of the central importance of love, so obvious in the mature novels, is blunted in the juvenilia by alien intrusions, perhaps under Branwell's influence, from the world of Angrian politics.

In their efforts to leave no stone unturned in Brontë studies, devotees of the juvenilia are obviously right to pay attention to these early writings, where, thanks to Wise and his policy of splitting up Brontë manuscripts for financial gain, so much basic work has yet to be done. But it is about time that it was recognised that so far as the prose juvenilia are concerned, closer study will reveal not fresh clues to the Brontës but instead a fresh trail of red herrings.

THREE

Poetry

The poetry of the Brontës occupies a position halfway between the juvenilia and the mature novels. Some of the poems were prepared for publication and published while the Brontës were engaged on their first novels. Some of Emily's poetry has obvious literary merit; the talent of Charlotte and Anne is less impressive, but it can, unlike the farrago of the juvenilia, be measured against conventional literary standards. The poems are what the juvenilia are not, something worth considering in their own right, and with the existence of printed versions we do seem at last on firm ground when considering questions of date, text, and authorship.

Unfortunately the problems we have found when discussing the juvenilia are just as apparent when we turn to the poetry. In the first place, it can hardly be allowed that all textual problems have been cleared up,[1] and the fact of publication is a complicating rather than a simplifying factor, since all the sisters in 1845, and Charlotte in preparing a second edition in 1850, revised the manuscripts of the poems before publication. The fact that many of Charlotte's poems were extracted from her juvenile prose writings means that we have the same difficulties about authorship and interpretation of her poems that we met in the juvenilia. Emily's poetry has received exhaustive textual study from C. W. Hatfield, and, although there are still some poems of which the authorship and date is uncertain, we can be fairly confident that we have in his edition a reasonably accurate account of what Emily wrote and when she wrote it.

It is Emily's poetry which poses the thorniest problems of

interpretation. Two obstacles stand in the way of any student of her poems. We do not know for certain how far her poems were subjective statements of her own feelings or objective statements of the feelings held by characters she had invented in making up her imaginary land of Gondal.[2] Nor do we know for certain enough about Gondal to gain any assistance in evaluating or elucidating Emily's poetry. Anne's poetry too has a connection with Gondal, and it is an added source of confusion that any interpretation of Gondal that we make for one sister seems inapplicable to the other.

Fortunately, as so often with Emily and Anne, the evidence about Gondal is so meagre that it is possible to exhaust it without much difficulty. Gondal is first mentioned in 1834 in the joint note of Emily and Anne stating cryptically "the Gondals are discovering the interior of Gaaldine."[3] It would seem natural to date the inception of Gondal to 1831 when Charlotte left home for Roe Head, but the earliest poem definitely associated with Gondal is dated 1837. In her 1837 note Emily says that Anne is "writing a poem beginning 'fair was the evening and brightly the sun'— I Agustus-Almedas life 1st v. 1–4th page from the last."[4] Anne's poem involving two characters with Gondal names has survived, but Emily's account of Agustus-Almeda's life, presumably in prose, has perished. In 1841 both Emily and Anne seem to refer to prose narratives of Gondal. Emily writes:

The Gondalians are at present in a threatening state but there is no open rupture as yet. All the princes and princesses of the Royalty are at the Palace of Instruction. I have a good many books on hand.

Anne at Scarborough with the Robinsons says:

I wonder whether the Gondalians will still be flourishing, and what will be their condition. I am now engaged in writing the fourth volume of Solala Vernon's life.[5]

In 1845, we have the longest references to Gondal. Emily in referring to an expedition by herself and Anne to York says:

During our excursion we were, Ronald Macalgin, Henry Angora, Juliet Angusteena, Rosabella Esmalden, Ella and Julian Egremont, Catharine Navarre, and Cordelia Fitzaphnold, escaping from the palaces of instruction to join the Royalists who are hard driven at present by the victorious Republicans. The Gondals still flourish bright as ever. I am at present writing a work on the first wars. Anne has been writing some articles on this and a book by Henry Sophona. We intend sticking firm by the rascals as long as they delight us which I am glad to say they do at present.[6]

One year before writing this note in February 1844, Emily had transcribed her poems into two notebooks, one of which was entitled *Gondal Poems*, but she had continued to add poems to both notebooks during the years 1844 and 1845. From the last three years of her life, however, only two poems, both of them in the Gondal notebook, survive.

Anne in 1845 is less optimistic about Gondal. She says:

Emily is engaged in writing the Emperor Julius's life. She has read some of it, and I want very much to hear the rest. She is writing some poetry too. I wonder what it is about.

Then a little later, after mentioning *Passages in the Life of an Individual*, usually assumed to be *Agnes Grey*, she adds:

We have not yet finished our Gondal Chronicles that we began three years and a half ago. When will they be done? The Gondals are at present in a sad state. The Republicans are uppermost, but the Royalists are not quite overcome. The young sovereigns, with their brothers and sisters, are still at the Palace of Instruction. The Unique Society, above half a year ago, were wrecked on a desert island as they were returning from Gaul. They are still there, but we have not played at them much yet. The Gondals in general are not in first-rate playing condition. Will they improve?[7]

On this note of questioning we can conclude our examination of information about Gondal; all that survives apart from this is the poems themselves and two papers in Anne's writing listing the names of Gondal characters and Gondal place names.[8] The prose notes with their references to the life of Agustus-Almeda, Solala Vernon, and the Emperor Julius, the last of which is expressly distinguished from Emily's poetry, would seem to indicate the existence of a considerable body of prose writing by Emily and Anne, analogous to the chronicles of Angria by Charlotte and Branwell. If we follow the analogy, this prose writing would form a loosely connected series of stories, with main characters appearing in different situations at different times: we can hardly expect a closely knit narrative to emerge. Still less can we hope to guess the nature of this prose narrative from the poetry that has survived. Owing to Emily and Anne's habit of prefacing some of their poems with the names or initials of the Gondal characters involved in them, the task of reconstructing Gondal is not quite as absurdly difficult as reconstructing Shakespeare's plays from the lyrics in them,[9] or, perhaps more pertinently, of reconstructing Charlotte's juvenilia from her poems, but it is still obviously impossible. A fair indication of how the Gondal poems are merely the tip of the iceberg is given by the lists of names of Gondal characters. Whereas the list of place names made by Anne does seem to recur in both sisters' poetry, neither Anne's separate list of characters nor Emily's list of 1845 appear to have much relevance to either sister's poems or to each other. Indeed it is a disturbing feature of Gondal that though Anne and Emily obviously worked closely together on Gondal in the manner of Charlotte and Branwell, we could not tell from their poetry that they were writing about the same subject.

Not a great deal of Anne's poetry has obvious connections with Gondal, and it is generally assumed that much of Anne's poetry, like that of Charlotte and Branwell, is obviously personal if not autobiographical. We would naturally be inclined to say the same of Emily's poetry, especially in view of her division of her poems in 1844 into two notebooks, and of her anger at Charlotte's discovery of some poems in 1845,[10] but Miss Ratchford in *Gondal's Queen* thinks that all Emily's poetry can be fitted into the Gondal pattern.

This thesis, together with the parallel thesis that with a few inconsistencies there is only one Gondal narrative framework, is unproved and unprovable. It relies in part on the circular argument that seems to bedevil Brontë studies. A poem is labelled as being a Gondal poem on internal grounds and fitted into a definite place into the Gondal story; this poem is found in the 1844 untitled notebook, and therefore it is proved that the 1844 untitled notebook contained Gondal poems, although there is no certain evidence that the poem was a Gondal one in the first place. The same is true of attempts to relate most of the Gondal poems to one central female character, a kind of female Zamorna, with as many loves and as many names. There are two main female characters in Emily's poems, of whom one is called either Rosina or Alcona or Rosina Alcona, the other A. G. Almeda or most commonly A.G.A. The identification of these two characters appears to rest upon the fact that they are both beautiful and much loved, carrying a train of destruction in their wake. Rosina Alcona is beloved by a similarly Byronic figure called Julius, who in two poems is connected with a character called Geraldine S. The assumption that Rosina Alcona and Geraldine are the same is obviously tenuous, since monogamy is hardly to be expected from Gondal characters, and the assumption that Geraldine is A.G.A.'s middle name is similarly speculative.

A.G.A. is never expressly mentioned as having anything to do with Julius, and the identification of her with Rosina Alcona rests on two poems by a character called Fernando de Samara of Areon Hall declaring his betrayed love for A.G.A. In a third poem an unnamed character, plausibly identified as Fernando because he lives at Areon Hall, addresses Alcona. But the poem hardly evokes the same mood as the poems to A.G.A.; and the identification of Alcona with A.G.A., dependent upon the assumption that Fernando, or strictly speaking the inhabitant of Areon Hall, could not twice be unfortunate in his loves, is highly conjectural.[11]

The identification of Rosina with A.G.A. is at the heart of Miss Ratchford's reconstruction of the Gondal saga; once we cast doubt on this, we must be doubtful about several other parts of the story, and it is best to admit that it is as impossible to construct one single story as it is unlikely that Emily herself, unlike Charlotte, thought of only one Gondal narrative. We would not get very far in reconstructing the plot of *Wuthering Heights* if we had only a few fragments of dialogue between characters confusingly named Catherine or Heathcliff or Linton. The confusion would be even greater if we had in some cases only initials or places of residence or character traits as means of identification. Three characters beginning with H live in Wuthering Heights; all at some stage are desperate men, eager for revenge; Hindley and Heathcliff suffer when Frances and Catherine die, Hareton and Heathcliff are placed in menial positions, Hareton and Hindley are deprived by Heathcliff of their ancestral rights. Like Lockwood we would get confused between Catherine Linton, Catherine Earnshaw, and Catherine Heathcliff. In trying to identify A.G.A. with Rosina

Alcona and refuting the possibility that two generations might be involved in the Gondal story, Miss Ratchford pays no attention to the two Catherines in *Wuthering Heights,* one of whom is born Catherine Earnshaw of Wuthering Heights, becomes Catherine Linton of Thrushcross Grange but wishes she had become Catherine Heathcliff and lived in Wuthering Heights, while the other is born Catherine Linton of Thrushcross Grange, becomes Catherine Heathcliff of Wuthering Heights, but plans to return as Catherine Earnshaw to Thrushcross Grange.

It would indeed be more than likely that anyone who only had a few isolated fragments of *Wuthering Heights* to work on would give an extremely confused account of what the story was about. Such a person would, however, have some advantages over anyone attempting to reconstruct Gondal. In spite of the confusing re-duplication of Christian names and surnames, there are very few characters in *Wuthering Heights,* whereas, as Emily's birthday note of 1845 and Anne's list of proper names show, Gondal is less sparsely inhabited. Finally, we do know that there is one story behind *Wuthering Heights;* we cannot know whether this is true of Gondal.

This is not to say that we can say nothing about Gondal. Obviously the same fierce emotions of unfulfilled love and desperate revenge that permeate *Wuthering Heights* are apparent in the Gondal poems, even if we cannot be exactly certain who loves whom or why he is seeking revenge. Indeed Miss Ratchford has done a considerable service to students of *Wuthering Heights* in drawing attention to the strongly moral tone of Gondal. Sin is sin, and tends to be punished in Gondal, whereas in Angria Zamorna's immorality tends to be condoned, if indeed the term immorality is appropriate in such an unreal world. This contrast between the sternly moral world of Gondal and unreal amoral characters in Angria should be stressed because it appears to contradict the generally accepted notion that, whereas Charlotte's novels are almost boringly moral, *Wuthering Heights* is an amoral book. The change in Charlotte is easy to understand: greater maturity, her experience with Monsieur Heger, her view of Branwell, and perhaps the fact that some of the more immoral juvenilia were written by Branwell, are all factors which explain the reversal in her position. It is less easy to find reasons why Emily should have moved in the opposite direction, and perhaps study of Gondal can direct us to an examination of the moral qualities in Emily's more mature work.

This said, it must be added that much of the ingenuity displayed in fitting the Brontës' poetry into a pattern, whether autobiographical or Gondalian, is misplaced, and all the ingenuity in the world cannot disguise the severe limitations of most of the poems as poems. Charlotte's poetry has rightly been ignored by even her warmest admirers;[12] Southey said she possessed the faculty of verse,[13] and her verses might be used as paradigms to distinguish verse from poetry. A gift for narrative, a monotonous regularity of rhythm, and a humdrum orthodoxy of sentiment are the main features of the bulk of her work, much of which was not published until long after her death and which, like the juvenilia, can be excused on the grounds that it was not intended for publication. The narrative poems, especially *Gilbert*, have a certain amount of Gothic horror behind them, and it is interesting for students of the novels to see the recurrence of the motifs of prophetic dreams, parted lovers, wrecks at sea, supernatural voices, and abandoned heroines all playing their parts, just as the poems about master and pupil have an interest for the biographer. But though Charlotte declared that she had more poetry in her than did the prosaic Jane Austen,[14] she kept her poetry for her prose writing; it is interesting to compare the trite poems on Anne's and Emily's deaths with the infinitely more moving biographical notice in the preface to *Wuthering Heights*.[15]

Anne's poetry cannot be dismissed quite so easily. Her inferiority as a novelist, the false trail of the Weightman love affair, uncertainties about the nature and extent of the Gondal element, and even the lack of a proper text have militated against a proper appreciation of her talent.[16] The adaptation of some of her poems as hymns has hardly helped her reputation, although it is undoubtedly true that her use of religious imagery, her simple rhythms, and her preference for rhymes ending with an open vowel makes such an adaptation easy. Hymns are not popularly associated with poetry, but they do have common factors, and additional evidence of Anne's interest in poetry that could be sung is provided by her music book, in which the songs of Moore played a large part.[17] The stridency of Moore, and for that matter of

Scott and Byron, is, however, less conspicuous in Anne's poetry than in her sisters'; religious themes, eighteenth-century poetic diction, and a delicate sense of rhythm prevent some of the worst excesses of the more rumbustious verse of both Charlotte and Emily.

The trouble about Anne's poetry, as with much eighteenth-century poetry, is that the thought behind it is not very profound. The Gondal poems, of which there are more than most commentators allow,[18] are not marred by the morbid excesses that disfigure Charlotte's and Emily's poetry, but the characters in them display stark emotions and conventional nobility. The love poetry, whether inspired by a real or an imaginary lover, is hardly inspiring; the conventional rhymes and diction make the sentiment commonplace, and, unlike Emily's poetry where repetition of a key word helps to hammer out the logical thought of the poem, Anne's repetition can become tedious.

> There was no trembling in my voice,
> No blush upon my cheek,
> No lustrous sparkle in my eyes,
> Of hope, or joy, to speak:
> But oh! my spirit burned within,
> My heart beat full and fast!
> He came not nigh—he went away—
> And then my joy was past. (SHEA., pp. 208–209)

Attempts to make Anne into a profound philosopher are bound to fail. The thought behind poems like "Views of Life" and "Vanitas Vanitatum, Omnia Vanitas" is that of Dr. Johnson in "The Vanity of Human Wishes," a resigned acceptance of God's will; but the poems lack the concrete force of Johnson. There are traces in some of the poems written towards the end of Anne's life of opposition to some of the doctrines Emily seems to be preaching both in her poetry and in *Wuthering Heights*. Emily's savage rejection of conventional pieties, and her exultation in any intense emotion, although and sometimes because it removed one from the triviality of the world, would appear to be countered by the mood of "The Three Guides" and "Self-Communion," where the difficulties of life are gently accepted as preparation for making our hearts immune to despair.[19] We can find this same opposition of thought in the novels of the two sisters, and it is an indication of the weakness of Anne's poetry and the strength of Emily's that our principal interest in Anne's poems is as a preparation for the novels, whereas Emily's can be judged in their own right.

Unfortunately, few have been prepared to consider Emily's poems as poems: they have been seen as sources for biographical speculations, Gondalian fantasies, or preludes to *Wuthering Heights*. Of those who have concentrated on trying to assess Emily as a poet, most have admitted that her talent is an uneven one, and have been prepared to discard all but a relatively few of her poems and poetical fragments.[20] Emily's own methods of composition, whereby she made fair copies of her earlier poems, would seem to indicate a similar process of selection, and we should not waste too much time in denouncing such early extravagances as

> O God of heaven! the dream of horror,
> The frightful dream is over now;
> The sickened heart, the blasting sorrow,
> The ghastly night, the ghastlier morrow,
> The aching sense of utter woe;
>
> The burning tears that would keep welling,
> The groans that mocked at every tear
> That burst from out their dreary dwelling
> As if each gasp were life expelling,
> But life was nourished by despair. (H., pp. 40–41)

The monotonous rhythm and monotonous gloom are repeated in many an early poem, although Emily never wastes words, lapses into conventional sentiments, or indulges in weak rhymes. Her narrative poems, like that describing Douglas's ride (H., pp. 77–80), have more vigour about them than those of Charlotte. The use of natural images never seems strained, although in the early poems contrasts between summer and winter, between calm joy and turbulent sorrow are a little too frequent to be convincing. Though words like "drear" and "dark" predominate, the tone of the poems is not always a savage one; there are glimpses of unearthly glory in the murk, although perhaps the best moments of Emily's early poetry come when a grim note suddenly punctures the mood of conventional happiness, as in the line "Then scorn the silly rose-wreath now." (H., p. 131)

Emily's use of the single unexpected, sometimes even the colloquial word, is the most obvious stylistic feature distinguishing her work from that of her sisters. The famous poem entitled "The Old Stoic" begins with a stanza which in spite of its skilful use of alliteration and assonance would be fairly trite were it not for the surprising phrase "lust of Fame" in the third line.

> Riches I hold in light esteem
> And Love I laugh to scorn
> And lust of Fame was but a dream
> That vanished with the morn. (H., p. 163)

Lust is more naturally associated or contrasted with riches and love than with fame; the total contempt for all three forms of human ambition is neatly spelt out in the single word which puts the slightly pompous first line, "Hold in light esteem," firmly in perspective. Likewise in the poem "Aye there it is! It wakes tonight," perhaps the most naked token of Emily's mystic veneration of her pantheistic duty and total rejection of earthly values, the last verse contains one surprising word.

> Thus truly when that breast is cold
> Thy prisoned soul shall rise,
> The dungeon mingle with the mould—
> The captive with the skies. (H., p. 165)

"Mould" is an unexpected intimation of man's mortality, and at first sight in spite of the alliterative and the chiastic effects, the principle reason for using this word would seem to be the need to find a rhyme for "cold." On the other hand "mould," while finely expressing the contempt for the world which this poem shows, can mean "form" or "model" as well as "corruption," thus preserving an antithetical as well as a chiastic structure in the last two lines, and stressing heavenly perfection as well as earthly imperfection in the poem.

Emily's greatest poems were written from 1845 onwards at a time immediately preceding or during the composition of *Wuthering Heights*. There are obvious similarities between the poetry and the novel, although both are difficult to interpret. The well-known "Remembrance" is an obvious reminder of Heathcliff's love for Catherine, although in this Gondal poem it is Rosina Alcona who remembers Julius Brenzaida, cold in the earth for fifteen wild

Decembers. There is a slightly softer mood about this poem than
there is in *Wuthering Heights*; Heathcliff hardly melts at all into
spring, but the poem has all the strength, the technical assurance,
and the complete integration of the natural and spiritual landscape that we find in Emily's novel.[21]

"Stars" is another poem that has been associated with *Wuthering Heights*,[22] the cool stars being linked with Edgar Linton and
the powerful blaze of the sun with Heathcliff; this and similar
associations with parallel pairs of lovers in the Gondal saga or with
the condition of England in the 1840s seem an unnecessarily crude
interpretation of a poem which acknowledges, as perhaps *Wuthering Heights* does, the strength of both the opposing forces, but
seems to give, as *Wuthering Heights* does not, the mystery and
the magic to the cool world of the stars. It would be better to
regard this poem as a straightforward account of the impossibility
of reconciling the world of reality and the world of imagination,
an account of a particular experience that has universal appeal in
spite of the occasional flaw, as when Emily compares herself
revelling in her dreams to a petrel, or when she talks of the
wakened flies, a slightly too humdrum reminder of life in un-
ventilated Haworth parsonage.

"The Philosopher" is less easy to equate with *Wuthering
Heights* or indeed with anything. The manuscript of the poem is
missing,[23] and we find it difficult to divide the dialogue between
the philosopher, who clearly speaks the dismal refrain, longing for
death, in the second and third verses, and his interlocutor, who
clearly speaks the first verse. It is presumably the philosopher who
after his sad refrain reiterates his plea for death to cease the
warring of the three gods within his breast, and it is someone else
who tells him of the vision of harmony he had had an hour ago,
a spirit who bends his dazzling gaze on the rivers and makes their
inky waters sparkle wide and bright. The philosopher then replies,
addressing his remarks rather confusingly to a seer, saying that he
had been searching for this resolving spirit all his life.

Even if we succeed in punctuating the poem correctly, interpretation is still difficult. The three gods and the three rivers may
derive from the imagery of the book of Revelation: in Anne's poem
"The Three Guides," which has been seen as an answer to "The
Philosopher," the three possible guides are described as the spirits

of Earth, Pride, and Faith, and Anne seems to be recommending Christian Faith as the solution to Emily's problem, and the final two lines of Emily's poem with its reference to "Vanquished Good, Victorious Ill" might suggest that Christianity is one of the warring gods. It is tempting to associate the three gods and the three rivers with the tripartite division of the soul in Plato's *Republic* or the threefold division of the personality by Freud, although there is no evidence that Emily had read Plato or could have anticipated Freud. In spite of this uncertainty, it is clear that Emily was painfully working her way towards a mystic vision of an ideal world in which all the stresses of life are meaningless and irrelevant. This vision is more confidently expressed in "No Coward Soul is Mine," and in the strange fragment of a Gondal ballad, "Julian M. and A. G. Rochelle," printed in 1846 as a separate poem, entitled "The Prisoner." The Gondal poem has all the faults of Emily's worst verse, with a boisterous rhythm in direct contradiction to the note of grim dreariness which the poem is meant to strike. Yet, just as some of Verdi's operas can rise to ineffable heights in the middle of barrel-organ tunes, so the six stanzas beginning "He comes with western winds" take us away from the comic world of tragic opera, the clank of Gondal chains, to the rare world of a genuine mystical experience. In "The Philosopher" death is seen as a relief from the agony of yearning for the mystical moment of resolution, whereas in "The Prisoner" the mystical vision seems to be a herald of Death, the ultimate resolver. Heathcliff in *Wuthering Heights* seems to go through a change in philosophy, very similar to these two poems: it is rather embarrassing to ask why Heathcliff does not commit suicide, and the two poems may provide part of the answer. It would, however, be unjust to the two poems to see them simply as guides to *Wuthering Heights*: English poetry in this period is weak, in poems like those of St. John of the Cross describing a mystical experience, but "The Philosopher" and "The Prisoner" do something to make up for this weakness.

"No Coward Soul" is an even finer statement of Emily's pantheistic vision. Written as it is without any punctuation, quite unlike anything else, though reverberating with echoes from eighteenth- and nineteenth-century poetry it stands as a fitting culmination of Emily's poetic work. It is dated January 2nd, 1846, and there is a note in Charlotte's handwriting saying these were the last lines Emily ever wrote. In fact we have two rather bad versions of a Gondal poem dated September 14th, 1846, and May 13th, 1848, and an undated poem which Charlotte published in 1850 as by Ellis Bell, "Often rebuked, yet always back returning." Hatfield suggests, since there is no manuscript of the poem, that Charlotte may have written it; her editorial revisions were fairly drastic, but this is not really evidence for Charlotte having taken such a liberty, and the style and quality of the poem remind us of Emily. The poem suggests a move from "old heroic traces" and "paths of high morality," slightly down to earth "where the wild wind blows on the mountain side," and this may correspond to Emily forsaking Gondal and deeply philosophical poetry for the world of *Wuthering Heights*.

Emily's abandonment of poetry in the last three years is one of those Brontë puzzles that is almost impossible to solve. One way of solving it would be to discover more poems written by Emily in this period, although Charlotte's comment on "No Coward Soul is Mine," in spite of its inaccuracy, would suggest that Emily did not write much poetry in this period. She did write some, and those who suggest that Charlotte's discovery of the poems in 1845 was such a traumatic experience for Emily that it killed the poetry in her[24] ignore the fact that she did write a few poems, including "No Coward Soul," after this date. The experience of preparing her poems for publication in May 1846 and then of submitting *Wuthering Heights*, well under way in April 1846 and apparently completed in July 1846, to various publishers may have occupied much of her energy, and both Branwell and Mr. Brontë were causing the sisters some difficulty at the time. It is possible that *Wuthering Heights*, originally intended as a one-volume novel, may have been revised in 1846 and 1847, and Emily may possibly have occupied her time with a second novel.

Equally puzzling is the relationship between *Wuthering Heights* and the poems.[25] Obviously there are similarities. The Gondal poems have a strong narrative thread behind them, and *Wuthering Heights* is a very poetic novel. Both poems and novel deal in extremes, wild despair being interspersed with unearthly joy. The landscape is generally rugged with isolated havens of calm beauty. And yet it would be a mistake to see the poems simply as a preparation for *Wuthering Heights*: to do so would be to do an injustice to the quality of the great lyrics, and to distort the meaning of the greater novel. The emotions expressed in "No Coward Soul is Mine" resemble those expressed by Catherine when she says "I am Heathcliff," but Heathcliff with all his faults is both a less satisfactory and more satisfying vehicle of love than the God within Emily's breast. In the poems we see Emily fretting over the same problems which she discusses in *Wuthering Heights* and offering varying solutions to them, but she does not, as she does in the novel, pit solution against solution and leave the greater problems unsolved.

FOUR

Wuthering Heights

Emily is the most inscrutable of the Brontë sisters, and we have very little information about the composition of *Wuthering Heights*.[1] It is usually assumed to have been written in the first half of 1846 at the same time as *The Professor* and *Agnes Grey*; the letters of Charlotte to Aylott and Jones in April 1846 and to Henry Colburn in July 1846 chart the progress of these three tales, apparently completed by the middle of the year. The absence of any poetry written by Emily after the beginning of the year would seem to suggest a change from poetry to prose, although the length of *Wuthering Heights* might indicate an earlier date for Emily's embarking on the work. On the other hand, as both of Charlotte's letters talk of three separate volumes, and *Wuthering Heights* is very much longer than *The Professor* and *Agnes Grey*, it seems quite likely that the original *Wuthering Heights*, submitted to Colburn, was shorter than the final published version, and that Emily in the latter half of 1846 and in 1847 revised her work; she wrote scarcely any poetry in this period, and, though there is no evidence for her revising her novel, this is scarcely surprising. Information about the composition of *Wuthering Heights* could only really have come from Charlotte, who might well have been sensitive about the decision of Anne and Emily to go their own way, a decision which would have involved Emily in lengthening her novel to meet the standard three-volume requirement. The suggestion that Branwell was partly responsible for *Wuthering Heights* is less likely, although Emily could have taken some of her brother's work and grafted it on to her own. Any such revision must have taken place before the middle of 1847, as the proofs of *Wuthering Heights* and *Agnes Grey* had been sent to Haworth before August.

It seems almost sacrilegious to suggest that *Wuthering Heights* could have existed in an abbreviated form, and perhaps this is why nobody has made the suggestion, in spite of the plethora of critical and speculative writing about *Wuthering Heights*. Great novels like *Middlemarch* can arise from small beginnings, and *Wuthering Heights* does with its two narrators and two generations seem to be the kind of novel which could have existed in a shorter form. It is true that the presence of Lockwood as a narrator and the story of the younger Catherine seem absolutely integral parts of the novel, although it is also true that no popular re-creation of *Wuthering Heights* has been able to cope with either of these features; they are also partly responsible for the early feeling that the plot of *Wuthering Heights* was a confused one,[2] and for the modern confusion about the meaning and interpretation of the novel.

Since the pioneer work of C. P. Sanger[3] in showing that *Wuthering Heights* was carefully planned and internally coherent, few have been in doubt about what happens in *Wuthering Heights*, although a précis of the plot without the aid of Lockwood and Nelly Dean does make the novel look rather ridiculous. It is, however, little help to know that Emily had her feet on the ground in describing what happened if we are still in the air about what these happenings mean, and the almost infinite variety of modern readings suggests that a definitive interpretation of *Wuthering Heights* is beyond our reach. With a few exceptions, such as the much quoted but little read article maintaining that Nelly Dean was the villain of *Wuthering Heights*,[4] most of the uncertainty about *Wuthering Heights* centres on the personality of Heathcliff. The novel ends with us in doubt as to whether the ghosts of Heathcliff and Catherine are still walking over the moor, or whether, as Lockwood piously imagines, all are at rest. In the face of this unresolved doubt it is not surprising that critics have not been able to make up their minds whether Heathcliff is hero or villain, worker or capitalist, whether Wuthering Heights is more homely or more grim than Thrushcross Grange, whether the love affair between Heathcliff and Catherine is asexual or incestuous, whether the novel is amoral or sternly moral, and whether its conclusion represents a defeat for all that Heathcliff is striving for or a victory.

The novel begins with Lockwood.[5] All the Brontës make the names of their characters work for them, and the stupidity and closed mind of Lockwood is soon apparent when he relates his trivial love affair, and tries to relate his petty concerns to the completely alien world of Wuthering Heights, where he makes a series of ridiculous mistakes. Few readers of the first chapters of *Wuthering Heights* have failed to despise Lockwood, or to acknowledge his usefulness as a narrator, in that the barren world of the moors seems both more plausible and more attractive when seen through the filter of his bogus sophistication. On his second visit he is caught in a snowstorm and forced to stay the night at the Heights. Here, after reading some rather baffling extracts from the elder Catherine's diary, he falls into an uneasy sleep; he dreams first of a nightmare sermon divided into 491 parts delivered by the Rev. Jabez Branderham and then of a pathetic child calling herself Catherine Linton trying to get in through the window.

With these dreams we are back in the world of the poems; the pictures of the sermon and the crying waif have great power, but are difficult to interpret.[6] The first dream has an almost comic quality, but would seem to be principally designed to show the folly and wickedness of conventional moral standards such as those Lockwood has been applying. Lockwood's cruelty in the second dream would suggest that he has not learnt this lesson, and that there is still a barrier, represented by the window, between him and the world of the moors, in which Catherine has been wandering as a waif for twenty years. Nelly Dean's narrative is in a sense the opening of this window, although Lockwood as a detached outsider is always looking at the events Nelly describes as it were through a window. It is odd that the waif should describe herself as Catherine Linton; the elder Catherine does not become Catherine Linton until she is grown up, and it is her daughter who is Catherine Linton as a child. The ghostly child says she has been wandering for twenty years; this interval does not exactly correspond to the time between Catherine's engagement to Edgar and the time of the dream (twenty-one years) or between her marriage and the dream (eighteen years) or between her marriage and Heathcliff's death (nineteen years). It is probable that Emily is here, as also on the occasions when Lockwood reads the names Catherine Earnshaw, Catherine Linton, and Catherine Heathcliff, deliberately confusing the two generations,[7] and that the child trying to get through the window refers to the younger Catherine as well as to her mother; the happy resolution at the end of the story occurs nineteen years after one Catherine dies, and the other is born.

Lockwood's cries after his second dream awake Heathcliff, and his confused explanations infuriate his host, who in spite of his uncontrollable grief manages to retain a superficial courtesy towards Lockwood, even accompanying him back to Thrushcross Grange. Heathcliff's treatment of Lockwood is a masterly touch: we first think, as Lockwood himself thinks, that this show of politeness, indicated by such gestures as sending Lockwood a brace of grouse and visiting him when he is ill, is an indication of Heathcliff's humanity. As we realise Lockwood's worthlessness and Heathcliff's cruelty to his own family, the politeness to Lockwood seems savagely ironical, and we tend to agree with Nelly Dean that Heathcliff is "rough as a saw-edge, and hard as whinstone" (WH., p. 34), but as the reasons for Heathcliff's cruelty are made clear, we find ourselves grudgingly admiring a man who, unlike those around him, is strong enough to carry on with ordinary life although inspired by extraordinary grief.

Nelly Dean is a more complex figure than Lockwood. She is much more involved than Lockwood in her own narrative, and occasionally, as when she justifies her educated speech or apologises for her intrusiveness, we feel a certain clumsiness in Emily's handling of her almost omniscient narrator. On the other hand Nelly's shifts of sympathy and her pious utterances of half-truths are vital features of Emily's wish not to pass final judgement on her characters. In addition, it has been generally recognised that the violence of emotions and sentiments expressed in *Wuthering Heights* is such that a narrator like Nelly Dean is needed to prevent this violence appearing impossible or comic. It is easy to see that Lockwood, who is silly and selfish, is almost totally wrong in his judgements. Nelly shows loyalty to her employers and old friends, speaks the language of Christianity, is sympathetic to those in distress, and reveals a strain of sturdy common sense. It is therefore much less easy to dismiss her as wrong, and yet the shifting pattern of her responses clearly shows that her views are inadequate in dealing with the abnormal situation at Wuthering Heights. The change from Lockwood to Nelly Dean as narrator is a further indication that we are dealing with an extraordinary world, which neither Lockwood's trivial mind nor Nelly's good sense can properly appreciate. Because Nelly is, much more than Lockwood, part of this world we are uncertain how to respond to her;[8] her advice and her actions often result in disaster, and her Christianity often seems as hypocritical as her far-from-truthful account of Heathcliff to his unfortunate son.

Nelly's story begins with the account of Mr. Earnshaw's visit to Liverpool, from which he returns with Heathcliff, whom he says he has found abandoned in Liverpool. Mr. Earnshaw's partiality for Heathcliff, whom he names after a son of his who had died, has prompted speculation that Heathcliff was his illegitimate son,[9] and the Byronic taint of incest is introduced to complicate the love of Catherine and Heathcliff. There is nothing in Heathcliff's gypsylike appearance to support that he has any Earnshaw blood in him, although family likenesses play a prominent part in the novel, nor does Nelly ever hint at any unworthy motive on Mr. Earnshaw's part. His act in rescuing Heathcliff would seem to be a piece of spontaneous Christian charity. The fact that Mr. Earnshaw, as Nelly says (WH., p. 342), is a good man whose harbouring of Heathcliff leads to such trouble just shows the ineffectiveness of Christian charity.

The spectre of incest in *Wuthering Heights* does, however, raise the question of sex in the novel. It is very tempting, especially with *Jane Eyre* in mind, to regard the love between Heathcliff and Catherine as strongly sexual, while Edgar Linton, who bears a superficial resemblance to St. John Rivers,[10] provides love without any element of sexual passion. Catherine first meets Edgar at the age of twelve, and her essentially asexual childhood love for Heathcliff begins to suffer at this point. In the powerful scene (WH., p. 130) which must recall Lockwood's vision where Catherine dreams that she is back at Wuthering Heights, she thinks of the last seven years of her life as a blank. The years of puberty from twelve to nineteen are the years in which the temporary attractions of Edgar Linton blind Catherine to her everlasting bond with Heathcliff, although in speech after speech to Nelly, Catherine seems aware of the mistake she is making. When Heathcliff returns, he and Catherine address each other at times in the words of ordinary lovers, and they part forever after a passionate embrace; but it would be to cheapen the impact of *Wuthering Heights* to imagine that this is an ordinary love affair. It is Edgar who displays conventional sexual jealousy, and ordinary romantic love receives short shrift in the novel, since it is satirised in Isabella's infatuation for Heathcliff. The unions of Heathcliff and Isabella and Catherine and Edgar result in children; the possibility of a sexual relationship between Heathcliff and Catherine seems a monstrous irrelevance. It is perhaps worth pointing out that the younger Catherine is conceived at the same time as Heathcliff returns from his three years' absence, but it is certainly worth pointing out that Catherine is seven months pregnant at the time of Heathcliff's last crushing embrace.

It is necessary to labour the point that, contrary to popular ideas about the novel, the love between Heathcliff and Catherine transcends the ordinary sexual love which Edgar shows and with which Nelly Dean sympathises. This is because, led by Nelly Dean, many critics have persisted in seeing Heathcliff as the alien stormy element destined to upset the calm which existed at Wuthering Heights before Mr. Earnshaw brought him home, and the calm which existed at Thrushcross Grange before he returns from his mysterious absence.[11] A much better case can be made out for saying that Heathcliff and Catherine have in their childish innocence established complete harmony, and that this is broken by a series of intruders. Even Nelly Dean seems to appreciate this harmony when she describes Catherine and Heathcliff comforting each other with thoughts of heaven after Mr. Earnshaw's death, and the religious imagery of heaven and hell is a recurring pointer to the deprivation both Catherine and Heathcliff feel when alien elements intrude.

The first such intrusion comes when Hindley returns home after his father's death, bringing with him a wife. Frances Earnshaw appears first as a silly and spoilt girl whom Nelly does not like because she is a stranger, but Nelly's attitude changes when Hareton is born, and Frances's gallant refusal to admit that she is dying wins her admiration. This is the first of many instances where Nelly's loyalties shift. There is of course nothing surprising in Nelly's initially being hostile to the stranger who has married the family's eldest son, and then favouring her when she in turn has produced an heir, especially as Nelly's links with Hindley Earnshaw are so strong (she is his foster sister). Nor is it surprising that Nelly, who initially shares the prejudices of Heathcliff against the Linton family as the spoilt inhabitants of an alien world, should eventually, while still retaining a distant loyalty to the Earnshaws, become dedicated to her new employers, the Lintons. But these changes in loyalty, while realistically acceptable to those who have had any experience of narrow village communities, do prepare us for the almost total refusal of *Wuthering Heights* to lay down moral judgements.

On the surface one of the least attractive characters in *Wuthering Heights* is Hindley Earnshaw. His treatment of Heathcliff is responsible for the sullen mood of revenge which soon builds up in the novel, and his drunken profligacy is unredeemed by any of Arthur Huntingdon's charm. His enthusiasm for promoting the marriage between Edgar and Catherine seems calculating, and his total neglect of Hareton seems deplorable. Yet Nelly Dean seems to accept the young Hindley's brutality as part of his role as master, and she is always ready to show sympathy with her old foster brother when he becomes a haggard reprobate. The reason for Hindley's collapse is the death of Frances; Heathcliff's return merely ensures that Hindley is financially as well as morally ruined. Nelly (WH., p. 191) ponders why the premature deaths of their wives should have affected Hindley and Edgar Linton so differently; on this occasion, her conventional piety would seem to overcome her loyalty to Hindley, as it could be argued that Edgar's melancholy retreat from the world is almost as selfish as Hindley's dissipation and that Hindley's love for Frances, although fairly shallow, was at any rate reciprocated, whereas the love between Edgar and Catherine had a much stronger competitor. Nelly does not compare Heathcliff's reactions towards Catherine's death with either Hindley's collapse or Linton's decline; however, the reader does, and, although Heathcliff gains in stature through not giving way to weakness, Hindley and Edgar gain a little because their lesser loves are enmeshed in the greater.

Although Hindley is hardly affectionate towards his sister, he does look like her, and there are associations between the two. Catherine resembles her brother in being monstrously selfish, and savagely petulant when she does not get her own way. She shows something of his shallowness and weakness in being won over by the slightly vulgar luxury of life at Thrushcross Grange. Yet she rises easily above this vulgarity, just as Emily rises above the banal story of a girl torn between a rich man she does not love and a poor man she does. Nelly preens herself on her careful catechism of Catherine's reasons for marrying Edgar; it is easy to see that Catherine's heart is not in her pert answers, although they seem to satisfy Nelly, who asks what is the obstacle to the marriage. Catherine explains that the obstacle is Heathcliff, and in a remarkable speech (WH., p. 82), part of which Heathcliff overhears, says that she dreamt that she was in heaven but felt that she had no business to be there, any more than she had any business to marry Edgar. It is Heathcliff she loves, "not because he's handsome—but because he's more myself than I am"; but she cannot marry Heathcliff because it would degrade her to do so.

According to Nelly, Heathcliff leaves when he hears Catherine say that she would be degraded. This is odd, because Catherine's next words are "he shall never know how I love him," and, unless Heathcliff had made a remarkably quick exit, or had been completely overcome by rage or misery, he could hardly have avoided overhearing these words and Catherine's statement that her soul and his are the same. It is possible that Emily, anxious to bring out the irony of Heathcliff's leaving just before Catherine makes the finest statement of her love for him, has forsaken realism at this point, or that Nelly has unconsciously put some of Catherine's sentiments in the speech in which she says, "Nelly, I *am* Heathcliff" (WH., p. 84), into the earlier speech declaring marriage with Heathcliff to be impossible. Emily is, however, a careful plotter, and we have no reason elsewhere to distrust Nelly's photographic memory. It seems more likely that Heathcliff does hear Catherine saying that he will never know how much she loves him, and does not care about this love, which presumably does not need to be uttered. What he cares about is marriage, and Catherine's refusal to marry him because of his menial position drives him out of the house for a mysterious period of three years, during which he loses his menial position and his chance to marry Catherine.

Emily's handling of this part of the narrative is faultless. After lingering on Catherine's declarations of love for Heathcliff and her desperation at his disappearance, she hastens over the next three years. We are left in doubt as to the reasons for the long delay in Catherine's marriage, and the reader, like Lockwood, can only speculate as to what Heathcliff was doing in the meantime. Nelly is anxious to conclude this section of her tale, and the reversal to Lockwood at this stage in the story is a useful device because it makes the shift in Nelly's loyalties less glaring. For in the next section of the narrative, full of incident, Heathcliff, bent on revenge, is definitely the enemy, and Linton, patiently putting up with Catherine's selfishness but unprepared to share her with Heathcliff, wins Nelly's respect. Catherine is still the same, and it is she who carries us through the next difficult six months in which Heathcliff returns, she falls ill, and Heathcliff elopes with Isabella. It is natural that Catherine should confide in Nelly, but Nelly seems to both know too much and do too little; Emily has on occasions to apologise for her presence, and some modern critics have shared Edgar's irritation with her.

The presence of Isabella as a complicating force in the plot is another hazard which Emily does not quite overcome. Like her son she has a certain pathos resulting from her total inability to appreciate Heathcliff's harsh ways. However, although an attempt is made to make her a sympathetic and credible character by allowing her to narrate the story of her return to Wuthering Heights, her long letter does not really give an insight into her character, but only into the grim atmosphere of the house. Even the evocation of this atmosphere, because it is created by a new narrator directly involved in the action, seems perilously strained. It is in Isabella's narrative that the resemblance between *Wuthering Heights* and Stella Gibbons's *Cold Comfort Farm* is most apparent. Isabella does perhaps gain a certain amount of sympathy when she returns briefly to Thrushcross Grange after Catherine's death, but by then the damage is done.

Another question hanging over this section of the book concerns the motivation of Heathcliff himself. It takes us some time to realise that he is inhumanly bent on revenge. Although he is initially more friendly to Nelly than Edgar Linton is, we are apt to consider Nelly's judgements on him as warped by conventional.

loyalty to her employer and to the marriage tie. Catherine, who in this section of the book as in the former is responsible for guiding us through uncharted areas of human experience, is soon aware of Heathcliff's inhumanity, and warns Isabella, "Pray, don't imagine that he conceals depths of benevolence and affection beneath a stern exterior! He's not a rough diamond—a pearl-containing oyster of a rustic: he's a fierce, pitiless, wolfish man" (WH., pp. 105–106). It is not wholly clear, however, why Heathcliff encourages Isabella, and finally elopes with her. Obviously Edgar, like Nelly, is distressed by such a dangerous match, but Heathcliff's desire to revenge himself on Edgar, like his desire to ruin Hindley, seems somehow only a fraction of his purpose. Isabella after her marriage is compared to a slut and a slattern (WH., pp. 153, 156), and obviously some degradation of the Lintons is part of Heathcliff's aim, but he is aiming higher than this. It would be more natural to explain Heathcliff's conduct with Isabella as part of his vengeance on Catherine. She has been untrue to their love by marrying someone conventionally attractive but inherently worthless, and Heathcliff does the same, Isabella Linton having all her brother's weaknesses and none of his redeeming qualities.[12]

Certainly the marriage between Isabella and Heathcliff, like the later marriage between Linton Heathcliff and the younger Catherine, is a hideous parody of the match between Edgar and Catherine. In arranging both marriages Heathcliff would seem to be punishing Edgar, who regards them as disastrous, but one would have though that Edgar had been sufficiently punished by the alienation of Catherine. In marrying Isabella, Heathcliff might seem to be revenging himself on Catherine, but he says he is not doing this, and significantly Catherine, who is already at death's door before Isabella elopes, never alludes to the actual marriage between Heathcliff and Isabella, although much earlier she had urged Heathcliff to take advantage of Isabella's infatuation for him.

One reason why this section of the novel is so discordant and so difficult to understand is that Heathcliff and Catherine, who ought to be in harmony with each other, are except at odd moments in fundamental disagreement. Catherine imagines, and for a time is happy in her illusion, that she can preserve her conventional marriage with Edgar and her total love for Heathcliff. Catherine maintains that the reappearance of Heathcliff has reconciled her to God and humanity, and sinisterly Heathcliff takes up the word humanity when he twice says that Edgar's "duty and humanity" is totally worthless (WH., pp. 154, 160). Catherine obviously has some feelings for Edgar Linton, although he is made to behave in a weak and conventional fashion; she is annoyed that he retires to his books when she is in despair, and complains "You are one of those things that are ever found when least wanted, and when you are wanted, never!" (WH., p. 132). Torn between Heathcliff's inhumanity and Linton's humanity, Catherine collapses and dies, here too forcing herself into conflict with Heathcliff's passionate desire that she should live. Catherine's dilemma is well shown in the symbolism and even the rhythm of the following delirious outburst to Nelly, when she is tearing the feathers from her pillow:

"That's a turkey's," she murmured to herself; "and this is a wild duck's; and this is a pigeon's. Ah, they put pigeons' feathers in the pillows—no wonder I couldn't die! Let me take care to throw it on the floor when I lie down. And here is a moor-cock's; and this—I should know it among a thousand—it's a lapwing's. Bonny bird; wheeling over our heads in the middle of the moor. It wanted to get to its nest, for the clouds had touched the swells, and it felt rain coming. This feather was picked up from the heath, the bird was not shot: we saw its nest in the winter, full of little skeletons. Heathcliff set a trap over it, and the old ones dared not come. I made him promise he'd never shoot a lapwing after that, and he didn't. Yes, here are more. Did he shoot my lapwings, Nelly? Are they red, any of them? Let me look." (WH., p. 126)

It is natural to associate Catherine with the wild birds, and especially the lapwings, while birds like pigeons represent the domestic circle of the Lintons which Catherine dislikes: Isabella has just been mentioned (WH., p. 114) as feeding some pigeons in the court. But Heathcliff's attitude to the lapwings and therefore to Catherine is ambivalent. We do not know if he shoots them, nor is the significance of setting the trap wholly clear, although we could say that Catherine is blaming Heathcliff for forcing her into the trap of marriage with Edgar, thus destroying her prospects of a fruitful marriage with Heathcliff. Yet a simple equation of the little skeletons with the unborn children of Heathcliff and Catherine is obviously too crude an interpretation of a passage where the pathetic melts into the macabre in the same way as the clouds touch the swells.[13] Nor, persuasive though Catherine's poetry is, should it blind us to the alternative case presented by Edgar with Nelly as his rather prosaic advocate or to the savage rhetoric of Heathcliff.

In spite of Nelly, Edgar Linton gains stature as the book advances. Charlotte's remark that he was an example of constancy and tenderness seems correct, ineffective though this constancy and tenderness is in finally saving Catherine. As a child Edgar seems spoilt, and in his first encounters with Heathcliff after his return he seems snobbish and childishly weak. His retreat to his library, and his concern for Isabella rather than Catherine, are further indications that ordinary duty and humanity, although admired by Nelly Dean, are ineffective and inappropriate. Yet he is Catherine's husband, whom at times she seems to need and even to love; his long period of mourning after Catherine's death and his affection for the younger Catherine do win us over to his side eventually.

There is thus a bond between Catherine and Edgar, and it is this bond which Heathcliff's outlandish behaviour before and after Catherine's death is aiming to sever. In claiming that he is not taking vengeance on Catherine, Heathcliff is telling the truth in that he wants the true Catherine, free as the moors, to be happy away from the restraints of Thrushcross Grange, but he ignores Catherine's affection for Edgar, and the only way he can show that this affection is shallow is by the mockery of his marriage with Isabella. It is at this point that Edgar shows himself at his most devoted, and thus when Heathcliff returns to claim his triumph he finds that Catherine can only gain her freedom through death. In their last passionate embrace Catherine and Heathcliff seem almost united, but he leaves her in Edgar's hands about to bear Edgar's daughter, and thus his victory is certainly unaccomplished.

After Catherine's death, described peacefully after the passion of the previous chapter, Heathcliff really comes into his own. Like Dostoevsky's Stavrogin, to whom he is often compared, Heathcliff's brooding presence is felt at a distance throughout the first

half of the novel, but unlike Stavrogin, Heathcliff fully lives up to
expectations when he finally emerges onto the centre of the stage.
It is true that after his outburst of anguish on Catherine's death
we do not see him for some time, except in the brief and biassed
account of Isabella when she comes to Thrushcross Grange to
announce her escape from Wuthering Heights. It is also true that
Heathcliff's malignity, difficult to explain before Catherine's death,
seems almost pointless after she has died; Hindley and Edgar are
both broken men; the vendetta against the younger generation
seems inexplicably cruel; Catherine cannot be won; and yet with
perverse logic Heathcliff carries out his mission.

Heathcliff's mission is still to win Catherine. On the one hand
in rather a masochistic way he seems to be competing with Edgar
in order to see which can suffer most on earth and thus win the
greater prize in heaven. This masochistic note is conspicuous in
some of Emily's later poetry, especially "The Visionary," and there
can be no doubt that as Heathcliff's anguish racks him more than
Edgar's, he seems destined for an earlier blessing, although it is
Edgar who dies first. Nelly Dean keeps at a distance from her
master, whose gentle melancholy she respects, but Edgar's inability to show his sorrow even to those fairly close to him is a
notable contrast to the conduct of Heathcliff, who is not afraid
to reveal his grief to Lockwood.

On the other hand Heathcliff is also striving with Edgar to win
possession of the younger Catherine. Nelly's motherly fretting over
Cathy's welfare and Edgar's mild affection are useless against
Heathcliff, who is determined to get Cathy for himself as the
representative of her mother and to ruin her because she is the
daughter of Edgar. Lockwood early in the book (WH., p. 11)
raises the possibility that Cathy may be married to Heathcliff, but
such a match, though not beyond Heathcliff's cunning, would
have been disloyal to the elder Catherine. Instead Heathcliff uses
his son Linton to gain control of Cathy, thus setting the seal on
his mockery of the marriage of Catherine and Edgar.

The engineering of the wedding of Cathy and Linton is thus a
masterly stroke on Emily's part as well as on Heathcliff's, since it
enables Heathcliff's revenge to become coherent. It may seem
unnatural that Cathy should even fancy herself in love with such
a feeble creature as Linton, and the actual marriage between them,

to which Cathy only consents because she wishes to see her father again, seems a little forced. Linton is by this time very ill, and he seems to combine on the occasion of his marriage something of his father's cruelty with the weakness of his mother's side of the family. In the early days of their acquaintance he is merely pathetic. Nelly comments on the grace of his appearance, Cathy calls him pretty, and life must have been dull for her at Thrushcross Grange, so that the love letters which Linton sends with the help of Heathcliff find a prompt response. Part of the attraction of Linton is that he lives at Wuthering Heights, to which Cathy, as her mother's daughter, is readily drawn, whereas Linton clearly would prefer life at Thrushcross Grange. When they compare their views on this idea of heaven Cathy wants "all to sparkle and dance in a gorgeous jubilee," Linton "all to lie in an ecstasy of peace" (WH., p. 257). This seems an obvious echo of the passage where the elder Catherine dreams she is thrown out of heaven, and wakes up on the moors near Wuthering Heights, sobbing for joy; it is natural to assume that the atmosphere at Wuthering Heights is meant to be more stormy than the more peaceful Thrushcross Grange.

The difference between the two houses is of major importance in the whole book's structure.[14] It is very easy to make too schematic a distinction and to maintain that all at Thrushcross Grange is peaceful, although the terrible scenes at Catherine's death occur there, or to maintain that all at Wuthering Heights is savage, although Heathcliff and Catherine enjoy happiness as children there, and Hareton and Cathy fall in love there before rather perversely moving house to Thrushcross Grange. It can be argued that Wuthering Heights shows a healthy organic yeoman's way of life and Thrushcross Grange the pampered artificial life of the gentry, although it is more usual to say that Wuthering Heights stands for savage inhumanity and Thrushcross Grange for civilised comfort. There are times, especially for Lockwood, when Thrushcross Grange provides a chilly welcome, and there are times, especially during Cathy's visits to Linton, when some added luxuries and even the weather contrive to make Wuthering Heights a haven of peace. This blurring of the distinction between the two houses of course explains how the oddly matched couple seem for a time to be partially suited to each other, although by the time of the forced marriage Linton's total unworthiness is all too apparent.

One of the first to detect Linton's spoilt nature is the old servant Joseph, whose lowering presence is a dominating feature at Wuthering Heights; he first appears on the second page and we last hear of him just before the novel's conclusion staying on at Wuthering Heights when Cathy and Hareton have abandoned it for Thrushcross Grange. Joseph does not initiate action, he only comments on it; and his comments are as sour as his language is rough and his theology harsh. In his role as spectator Joseph resembles Nelly Dean and Lockwood, but whereas Nelly Dean is prepared to give both praise and blame, and Lockwood rarely finds fault, Joseph, apart from a certain atavistic loyalty to Hindley and Hareton, condemns almost everyone in the book. Thus Joseph's hostility to Linton for despising his porridge is less effective, as he blames even Nelly Dean for frivolity, and there is scarcely a character in the book whom he does not see destined for damnation. This enthusiasm for hellfire may seem so repellent as to be almost comic; neither Joseph's narrow personality nor his crabbed theology with its Calvinist undertones seem at all in accordance with the philosophy of Emily Brontë. And yet there is a sense in which, just as Lockwood is totally wrong in passing judgement too rapidly and favourably on the inhabitants of Wuthering Heights, and Nelly Dean is partially wrong in her conventional wisdom that distributes an equal measure of praise and blame, Joseph was felt by Emily to be right in finding almost everything as worthless as withered weeds. Certainly it is the function of the house Wuthering Heights, as it is of the book to which it gives its name, to challenge all normal standards.

And yet it would seem that there is a return to normality with what looks like the happy ending of a fairy story. Heathcliff, the wicked uncle, dies, and Cathy, the beautiful heroine, is free to marry the hero, Hareton, who has a heart of gold beneath a rugged exterior. Just to make the fairy story even more decorous, the wicked uncle shows signs of relenting before he dies. In fact, what makes the story a very unusual one is that it is Heathcliff who plays the major role, and we are so interested in his excitement at the prospect of approaching death that the growing love between

Cathy and Hareton seems of secondary importance. This secondary love story is of course relevant to the story of Catherine and Heathcliff in that Cathy's presumably happy marriage to Hareton, whom she originally regards as her social inferior in contrast to the superficially attractive Linton, is a reminder of how the elder Catherine should have behaved towards Heathcliff and Edgar. And yet this reminder, which would be so poignant as the love story of the two generations is brought to a conclusion, is blunted by Cathy and Hareton abandoning Wuthering Heights for Thrushcross Grange.

Both the move away from Wuthering Heights and the whole story of the love between Cathy and Hareton have been something of an embarrassment to critics of the novel.[15] There have been some interesting but rather narrow sociological explanations of the departure from Wuthering Heights, seen as the forsaking of the traditional yeoman's way of life; Hareton's attempts to replace the currant bushes by flowers has been interpreted as a sign of the times, although those who emphasise this episode do not notice that his attempt is unsuccessful.[16] It is easier to see the departure to Thrushcross Grange as in some way a defeat for Heathcliff, and all that he has striven for, in the same way that on his own admission Cathy and Hareton defeat all his attempts to destroy the family of Hindley and Linton.

Some have tried to strengthen this conclusion by saying that Cathy and Hareton are the children of love, or that they are the legitimate final representatives of a closely knit family tree, where it is Heathcliff who is the outsider.[17] Such a view exaggerates the love between Hindley and Frances, and between Catherine and Edgar, which cannot stand comparison with that between Heathcliff and Catherine. Nor, though commentator after commentator on *Wuthering Heights* draws up the family tree of the Earnshaws and Lintons, and remarks upon its extraordinary symmetry, is there anything really remarkable in the marriage of Cathy to her two first cousins; in Victorian society with its keen sense of social and moral decorum, there were plenty of marriages between first cousins, and it would be possible to trace similar symmetrical patterns in the family trees of the Brontës' own few friends. It is true that Lockwood sees the words Hareton Earnshaw inscribed over the door of Wuthering Heights[18] when he first goes there, but this does not mean that Hareton is bound to inherit Wuthering Heights (in fact he abandons this inheritance).

It is natural for Cathy and Hareton to fall in love, given that their essential good nature is not totally warped by their harsh upbringing. Yet Heathcliff with his powerful hold over Hareton's affections and Cathy's whole life could have thwarted the love affair if he had wanted to do so. Thus it is difficult to speak of a victory of Cathy and Hareton over Heathcliff, since it is Heathcliff who seems partly responsible for the victory, and in any case it is in Heathcliff's passionate love affair with the ghost of Catherine rather than the more tepid romance between Cathy and Hareton that the interest of the last few chapters of the story lies.

When Lockwood leaves Heathcliff for the last time, Cathy has just rejected Hareton's clumsy overtures, and there is not much more than a hint that she will ever be moved by them. Indeed Lockwood's final remark before he leaves Thrushcross Grange is that it would have been a "realisation of something more romantic than a fairy tale" (WH., p. 316) if he and Cathy had struck up an attachment. One of the problems about the last section of the novel, and it is possibly a weakness as well, is that we are in doubt whether Lockwood has learnt from his experiences or not. He is hardly a sadder or a wiser man if he is really still thinking that a marriage with Cathy was a possibility, but in fact his words suggest that such a match would be impossible, and there is a certain irony about the words "romantic" and "fairy tale" which casts a shadow on the slightly more realistic match between Cathy and Hareton.

Before Lockwood leaves, there are signs that Heathcliff is beginning to relent when he displays some affection towards Hareton on the occasion of Cathy's scorning him. Hareton looks like Catherine, and is in the same menial position as Healthcliff had been; Heathcliff recognises this (WH., p. 336), and would indeed have had to be inhuman not to sympathise with him. As Charlotte Brontë saw, "the single link Heathcliff has with humanity is his rudely-confessed regard for Hareton" (WH., p. lvii). After Lockwood leaves, Hareton makes more progress in winning Cathy's affection, and Heathcliff moves gradually towards his death and reunion with Catherine.

It has been argued that when Cathy and Hareton ruin Heathcliff's revenge, he has no reason for living, but signs of Heathcliff's relenting appear well before his startlingly rapid final decline. It seems more probable that it is Heathcliff's relative kindness towards Cathy and Hareton which is the agent of his redemption from a life of torment. This is not made expressly clear, although the juxtaposition (WH., p. 335) of the passage in which Heathcliff says that after all his labours he cannot exert himself to destroy Cathy and Hareton and his announcement that he feels a strange change approaching must be significant. At this time, however, he is still strong and healthy, and he does not have much contact with any other inmate of Wuthering Heights. His deliberate avoidance of Cathy and Hareton's presence may mean something; with his thoughts on the elder Catherine, he suggests that this is because they remind him too painfully of her, but it may be that he is anxious to avoid the temptation of completing his vengeance. Heathcliff does talk rather wildly of summoning his lawyer, Mr. Green, but we are left in some doubt as to whether he had intended to get Green to disinherit Hareton and Cathy, or whether he had wished to make everything right by duly leaving to them by his will what they would inherit anyway.

It is true that Nelly Dean, ever anxious to pour conventional oil on the troubled waters of her story, sees no sign of any connection between Heathcliff's treatment of Cathy and Hareton, and his rediscovery of Catherine. The tale of Heathcliff's last four days on earth is an extraordinary achievement; it is told by the uncomprehending Nelly to the unsympathetic Lockwood, and yet Heathcliff's savage and unearthly blend of joy and grief is totally acceptable. One of the most remarkable traits of his behaviour, which distinguishes his outbursts from similar visionary experiences in the poetry, is his ability to bring himself down to earth and give practical directions. It is not, however, surprising that there are still some ambiguities about Heathcliff's death which can never be solved. There is no realistic explanation of why he died so rapidly, nor can we ever really be sure why his release from torture comes so soon.

Nor can we be sure whether Heathcliff is finally reunited to walk the moors with Catherine, as a little boy blubbers, or whether we should, like Lockwood gazing at the graves of Catherine,

Heathcliff, and Edgar, wonder "how any one could ever imagine unquiet slumbers for the sleepers in that quiet earth" (WH., p. 350). The note of peace on which the novel ends gives an appropriate cathartic effect, but just because Emily Brontë is right in striking this note, there is no reason to believe that Lockwood is necessarily right in denying the vision of Catherine walking on the moors. There is a faint reminder in this contrast of the two visions of Linton and Cathy's quarrel over the nature of heaven, but it is possible to work out a compromise between the little boy and Lockwood. Catherine and Heathcliff are walking the moors together; this for them is the peace they have been seeking.

Like almost every character in the book, Heathcliff can be defended as a character of superhuman energy transcending normal moral rules, or more conventionally attacked as a creature of the utmost cruelty and brutality.[19] Those who attack him sometimes seek refuge in the verdict of Charlotte as expressed in her 1850 preface to *Wuthering Heights*. According to Charlotte Heathcliff stands unredeemed (WH., p. xv), but she then qualifies this remark by saying that he betrays one human feeling, his affection for Hareton, and she then adds to this Heathcliff's friendliness towards Nelly Dean. In her final paragraph, however, she seems, possibly unconsciously, to weaken her hostility to Heathcliff once again.

Wuthering Heights was hewn in a wild workshop, with simple tools, out of homely materials. The statuary found a granite block on a solitary moor; gazing thereon, he saw how from the crag might be elicited a head, savage, swart, sinister; a form moulded with at least one element of grandeur—power. He wrought with a rude chisel, and from no model but the vision of his meditations. With time and labour, the crag took human shape; and there it stands colossal, dark, and frowning, half statue, half rock: in the former sense, terrible and goblin-like; in the latter, almost beautiful, for its colouring is of mellow grey, and moorland moss clothes it· and heath, with its blooming bells and balmy fragrance, grows faithfully close to the giant's foot.

The heath with its blooming bells at the foot of the crag reminds us of the heath and the harebells at the end of *Wuthering Heights*, but it must remind us, too, of the name of *Wuthering Heights*'s hero. At first sight the name Heathcliff in both its parts is harsh and barren, but the heath beneath the cliff in Charlotte's preface reminds us that there is beauty even in Heathcliff. Charlotte's uncertain response has been followed by many modern commentators. Like Shakespeare's plays, to which it is often compared, *Wuthering Heights* is capable of so many interpretations that each new approach has a certain freshness about it, while obviously failing to give the final answer. By distorting ambiguities into certainties, by concentrating on one nexus of interrelated images to the exclusion of all others, critics can reach a view of *Wuthering Heights* that is both partial and perverted;[20] any attempt to give a total picture of *Wuthering Heights* is bound to be incoherent, because in the last resort *Wuthering Heights* is incoherent. Virginia Woolf was right when she said of *Wuthering Heights*:

She looked out upon a world cleft into gigantic disorder and felt within her the power to unite it in a book. That gigantic ambition is to be felt throughout the novel—a struggle, half thwarted but of superb conviction, to say something through the mouths of her characters which is not merely "I love" or "I hate," but "we, the whole human race" and "you, the eternal powers . . ." the sentence remains unfinished.[21]

FIVE

Agnes Grey

Agnes Grey, apart from George Moore's startling claim that it was the most perfect prose narrative in English literature, has been treated on the whole with condescending indifference.[1] Biographers in spite of several indications to the contrary have seized upon *Agnes Grey* as a faithful portrait of Anne's years as a governess, but critics have largely followed early reviewers in either ignoring Anne's first book altogether or passing over it in a few sentences. *The Tenant of Wildfell Hall*, even if it had no merit of its own, would be worth studying because of its close connections with other Brontë novels, but *Agnes Grey* does not have these connections, and must stand or fall on its own merits.

The date of *Agnes Grey*'s composition is not known, although we know it was completed by July 1846. In her birthday note of 1845 Anne writes that she has begun the third volume of *Passages in the Life of an Individual*. The date of this reference and the episodic nature of *Agnes Grey* have naturally led to the identification of *Passages in the Life of an Individual* with *Agnes Grey*, but this identification must not be taken for granted. The birthday note is full of references to Gondal, and *Passages from the Life of an Individual* might be another Gondal saga like the book by Henry Sophona, mentioned by Emily in her birthday note. Nor is *Agnes Grey* long enough to be easily divisible into three volumes. In April 1846, when Charlotte wrote to Aylott and Jones announcing that Currer, Ellis, and Acton Bell were preparing three works of fiction, and again in July 1846 when she wrote to Colburn announcing that the novels were completed, *Agnes Grey*, together with *The Professor* and *Wuthering Heights*, were seen as one-volume novels.[2]

Agnes Grey could have been written in 1845–1846 in the twelve months between the time Anne left Thorp Green and the time Charlotte wrote to Colburn, just as Charlotte wrote the longer *Jane Eyre* in the year 1846–1847. If we identify *Agnes Grey* with *Passages in the Life of an Individual*, it was obviously begun much earlier and took much longer. The identification has undoubtedly contributed to the view that *Agnes Grey* is an episodic and auto-biographical work, a kind of running diary that Anne wrote about her experiences as a governess. If we do not accept the identification, then we are more likely to regard *Agnes Grey* as a more mature work, possessing some organic unity, without the auto-biographical streak that writers on Anne Brontë have persisted in finding in it.

Agnes Grey begins with a description of the Grey family. Agnes Grey's father is a clergyman with some small private means, her mother a rich squire's daughter, cast off by her family for marrying beneath her. The Greys live happily until Mr. Grey in trying to increase his private income loses all his capital. To redeem the family fortune Agnes decides to become a governess. Her first post with the cold-hearted, vulgar Bloomfields is a disaster. The young children with whom she has to deal are wholly unmanageable, and the Bloomfield parents provide no help in dealing with them. Dismissed from this post Agnes takes up another position with the Murrays, who are of a higher social position than the Bloom-fields. Their children are older, and on the whole Agnes is more successful in dealing with them, although the Murray parents, like the Bloomfields, continue to blame Agnes for the behaviour of the children, which is largely the result of their own shortcomings.

The most interesting character of the book is the eldest Murray daughter, Rosalie. Spoilt, selfish, and pretty, she has a train of male admirers, and even Agnes is drawn to her, although she hardly misses an opportunity to point out her faults. After inciting the frivolous rector Mr. Hatfield to make love to her and flirting rather unsuccessfully with Mr. Weston, the virtuous curate, Rosalie eventually accepts the proposal of Sir Thomas Ashby, although she continues to behave flirtatiously with all and sundry until her marriage. Shortly after the marriage Agnes, who has now fallen in love with Mr. Weston, is summoned home to hear that her father is dead, and after a little more time at the Murrays, in which she sees all too little of Mr. Weston, she moves with her mother to start up a school. Here she eventually meets Mr. Weston, and all ends happily for Agnes; this is in strong contrast to Rosalie Murray's unhappiness in marriage to the brutal Sir Thomas, which is described when Anne visits the Ashbys shortly before her reunion with Mr. Weston.

Like Anne Brontë, Agnes Grey was a governess who served two employers, and, like most governesses, she was not very happy with her employers. Agnes Grey's family is poor like Anne's and rather snobbish, but otherwise very different from her creator's. We do not know a great deal about the Inghams of Blake Hall, but they do not seem to have been very like the Bloomfields, possibly based in part on Charlotte's employers, the Whites. We know quite a lot about the Robinsons of Thorp Green, and they do not seem at all like the Murrays. Agnes falls in love with a clergyman, Mr. Weston, and Anne may or may not have fallen in love with another clergyman, Mr. Weightman, but between the grave Mr. Weston of the novel and the merry, flirtatious, and unfortunately dead curate of Haworth, there is a wider gap than even wish fulfilment can fill. Agnes's experiences with her employers may be based on fact, although possibly Anne was less successful than Agnes in coping with her recalcitrant charges. Similarly the attitude of Agnes towards her employers and towards the governess question may be a reflection of Anne's own attitude, although, as has been pointed out,[3] there is a distance between Agnes and her creator, who does not hesitate to point out Agnes's immaturity.

Supporters of an autobiographical interpretation of *Agnes Grey* have pointed to the statements both of Charlotte and of Anne herself defending *Agnes Grey* against the charge of exaggeration on the grounds that parts of the narrative were drawn from real life.[4] They also draw attention to the claims of Agnes herself at the beginning of the novel to be reciting a true story. This latter point is very weak, since Anne was obviously influenced by eighteenth-century novelists like Defoe and Richardson, who made similar claims that they were telling the truth. Charlotte is an unreliable witness where Anne is concerned, being too eager to defend her memory, while perhaps unconsciously deprecating her art. Anne's own words in her preface to the second edition of *The Tenant of Wildfell Hall* only say that parts of the narrative of *Agnes Grey* are drawn from life: they do not say whose life, and they do not say which parts.

If we deny that *Agnes Grey* is an autobiographical novel, it immediately becomes difficult to see what justification there is for making the novel so episodic. In particular the three chapters dealing with the Bloomfields are hard to explain. It is a feature of other Brontë novels that they begin with what seem to be a false start, although only in *The Professor* does the apparent false start not contribute obviously to enriching the rest of the novel. Even in *The Professor*, although the episodes with Edward Crimsworth do not seem to have much bearing on the scenes in Brussels, they do introduce one character, Hunsden Yorke Hunsden, who has some part to play in the latter half of the book; but the Bloomfields, who have held the stage in all their comic horror, then vanish without further mention.

It could be maintained that the Bloomfields are present in the novel to act as a foil to the Murrays, and indeed there are several obvious contrasts that can be drawn between the two households. The difference between the nouveau riche vulgarity of Wellwood and the stately grandeur of Horton Lodge is more than once emphasised, but the inhabitants of Horton Lodge are no real improvement. Mr. Murray, who is rarely seen, may seem slightly better than the ever-present interfering Mr. Bloomfield, but the cold-hearted, hypocritical, loquacious Mrs. Murray is probably meant to be the inferior of Mrs. Bloomfield, who for all her taciturnity and coldness of manner does seem to have some interest in her children's welfare. Agnes of course gets on better with the Murray children than with the Bloomfield children, but this is because they are older. As Anne herself makes clear, the dreadful Bloomfield children would in time calm down:

Every month would contribute to make them some little wiser, and, consequently, more manageable; for a child of nine or ten as frantic and ungovernable as these at six or seven would be a maniac. (AG., p. 386)

Thus one function of the Bloomfield chapters is to show us a badly-brought-up family at an earlier stage than we see the self-indulgent Murrays. What Anne appears to be saying is that the seeds of selfishness, thoughtlessness, and wickedness are sown early. At times she seems almost to be like Carus Wilson in her sinister denunciations of childish peccadilloes, as in her chilling attack on the third Bloomfield child, Fanny, who is barely four.

I found her a mischievous, intractable little creature, given up to falsehood and deception, young as she was, and alarmingly fond of exercising her two favourite weapons of offence and defence: that of spitting in the faces of those who incurred her displeasure, and bellowing like a bull when her unreasonable desires were not gratified. (AG., pp. 385–386)

There would be sufficient reason for including the Bloomfield chapters if *Agnes Grey* was just a novel about the right and wrong way to bring up children. At times it does seem to have this didactic aim, as when Agnes is made to say rather primly:

If a parent has, therefrom, gathered any useful hint, or an unfortunate governess received thereby the slightest benefit, I am well rewarded for my pains. (AG., p. 389)

But the novel is no mere narrow pedagogic treatise. For one thing it is clearly not only telling us how to treat children, but also how to treat governesses, and here the very different, but equally reprehensible, behaviour of the Bloomfields and the Murrays towards Agnes reinforces the moral that governesses should be treated as human beings and not as objects of convenience. Mrs. Bloomfield welcomes Agnes with numbing coldness, Mrs. Murray does not welcome her at all; by contrast, Agnes's mother would give a friendly welcome even to a servant girl. One cannot help feeling that the prickliness of governesses in general, and of the Brontë sisters in particular, slightly weakens this aspect of the novel; at times *Agnes Grey* appears not to be saying that governesses should be treated as human beings, but that there should not be governesses.

However, *Agnes Grey* is not just a governess story. The flirtations of Rosalie Murray, the love affair with Mr. Weston, and the strong element of religious propaganda, seen particularly in chapters like "The Cottagers," pages of which read like a religious tract or one of Mr. Brontë's edifying moral tales, have little to do with children or governesses, and we can return to the charge that *Agnes Grey* is episodic and disjointed, since there is little in the Bloomfield chapters that prepares us for either love or religion. It would also be true to say that both the religious chapters and the love affair with Mr. Weston are distinctly embarrassing to read. By contrast, Rosalie Murray's amours are light relief, and she becomes the main focus of the novel. There appears to be a dogmatic tendency in Anne, whereby some characters like Agnes herself, her family, and Mr. Weston are poor, serious, and unselfish, whereas others like the Bloomfields, Murrays, and their friends are rich, frivolous, and selfish. The novel ends with the good rewarded and the evil punished; this is unrealistic, and we are not even persuaded that Mr. Weston is good and Rosalie Murray is evil. Agnes waxes highly indignant at Rosalie's thoughtless flirtation with Mr. Weston, but never seems to complain at the latter's inexplicable neglect of her.

One way to defend Anne against the charge of being both disjointed and schematic in her ranging of black against white is to take a look at Agnes Grey's family. These are usually taken to be models of domestic happiness, the dutiful daughters Mary and Agnes being a wonderful contrast to the spoilt children Agnes later encounters, while Mrs. Grey, who is disinherited by her father for marrying a clergyman and yet is perfectly happy, is a useful reminder that Rosalie Murray should have preferred the charming Mr. Hatfield to the vicious Sir Thomas Ashby. A slight cloud hangs over Mr. Grey; it is, after all, his fault that in attempting to improve the family fortunes he brings penury to the Greys, and effectively causes Agnes to become a governess. Nor is he as buoyant or cheerful in facing up to these misfortunes as are his wife and daughters. Like Mrs. Gaskell, another unconsciously feminist writer,[5] Anne Brontë seems all too eager to blame misfortunes on men, and praise women for their courage in facing up to them. Mr. Grey is rather like Mr. Hale in *North and South:* in a sense his financial speculations are less pardonable than the theological speculations which impelled the Hales to leave their comfortable home.

In neither case are Mr. Hale or Mr. Grey ever really attacked for what they have done, but perhaps this omission makes the point more tellingly. There is some rather heavy-handed irony about Mr.

Grey's kind friend, "a man of enterprising spirit and undoubted talent who 'generously' proposed to give Mr. Grey a fair share of the profits and thought he might 'safely' propose that this share would be a considerable one," and this irony draws attention to certain unsatisfactory features about the Grey household which make it less easy to set it up as the polar opposite of the dreadful families to which Anne is governess.

Mrs. Grey, though obviously an admirable woman, capable, kind, and uncomplaining, is not without her weaknesses as a mother. This is stated very early on in the book:

My mother, like most active, managing women, was not gifted with very active daughters: for this reason—that being so clever and diligent herself, she was never tempted to trust her affairs to a deputy, but, on the contrary, was willing to act and think for others as well as for number one; and whatever was the business in hand, she was apt to think that no one could do it so well as herself. (AG., p. 361)

There is an ambiguity, probably unconscious, about the phrase "gifted with very active daughters." Mrs. Grey does not have very active daughters, but she would not be much good with them if they were active, and indeed when Agnes suggests becoming a governess, after the initial wave of disapproval, Mrs. Grey does not succeed in finding very good situations for her daughter. One would have thought that her own experience as a squire's daughter, moving in circles where governesses were common, would have persuaded Mrs. Grey to be more cautious in exposing her daughter to the mercies of the Bloomfields and expecting the more aristocratic Murrays to be kinder employers. She also might have done more to disillusion Agnes of the naive idealism with which she approaches her first post, "full of bright hopes and ardent expectations."

The really damning remark from the Grey family comes from Agnes's sister Mary, who, when Agnes offers to help her, tells her to go and "play with her kitten." Playing with a kitten is poor preparation for life as a governess, or indeed life in general, and one sometimes feels Anne may be saying that the gentle secluded education of the Grey girls is almost as unsatisfactory as that provided by the Bloomfield and Murray families.

In one of his few positive statements, Mr. Weston declares

that the "human heart is like india-rubber; a little swells it, but a great deal will not burst it. . . . Every blow that shakes it will serve to harden it against a future stroke" (AG., p. 465). As critics have pointed out,[6] Mr. Rochester uses the same simile, and there are other similarities between the two heroes: they share the same Christian name, have the same fine voice and rugged looks, are the object of some nearly idolatrous love on the part of the heroine, are pursued by a more aristocratic admirer, but eventually are reunited with their true love after a long absence. It is of course absurd to imagine Mr. Weston with a mad wife, proposing a bigamous marriage, although one cannot help wishing, rather irreverently, for him to show something of Mr. Rochester's dynamic strength. The resemblance between the two heroes does, however, serve to show that Mr. Weston is not just a static good angel to be placed in opposition to bad angels like Mr. Hatfield, whom we have shown is set up as a great deal better than Sir Thomas Ashby. He is also an active force, as are the whole of Agnes's experiences with the Bloomfields and Murrays, in educating Agnes in the ways of the world.

The early critic who declared that *Agnes Grey* was a coarser imitation of the works of Jane Austen[7] should make us aware of the possibilities of interpreting *Agnes Grey* as a Bildungsroman. Like Emma Woodhouse, Agnes Grey becomes gradually, through bitter experience, disillusioned with the false preconceptions which her comfortable life has given her. Less subtly than Jane Austen, Anne Brontë exposes these illusions in the contrast between Agnes's idealistic notions of her role as governess and the harsh realities of life at the Bloomfields, a very necessary stage in Agnes's education. By the time Agnes gets to the Murrays she is considerably more experienced, and we are able to contrast her good sense with Rosalie Murray's silliness.

Rosalie Murray is surrounded by illusion. She deludes Mr. Hatfield into making an untimely proposal to her, she deludes herself about her real feelings for him, she starts an improbable flirtation with Mr. Weston which is a sheer fantasy on her part, and eventually having kept her engagement quiet until the last possible moment she achieves her ambition and becomes Lady Ashby of Ashby Park, only to find herself miserable at the end of the novel. Fortified by experience, Agnes is sometimes prepared to tell her the truth, and Rosalie clings to her for this reason, although we cannot say that she has learnt a great deal by the end of the book. Agnes still pities her for her false idea of happiness which consists of pleasure and enjoyment.

Rosalie Murray is a good portrait of a butterfly, sacrificed as a result of her own illusions, but unfortunately Anne rather weakens the force of this portrait by making Agnes undergo similar illusions about Mr. Weston. Of course Mr. Weston turns out not to be an illusion; he returns, proposes honourable marriage, and unlike the Ashbys the Westons live happily ever after. But Mr. Weston hardly gives Agnes much encouragement while he is at Horton Lodge: the gift of bluebells is made as a simple act of goodwill, without compliment or remarkable courtesy, or any look that could be construed into "reverential, tender adoration," but it is enough to raise Agnes's hopes:

> Shallow-brained cheerfulness, foolish dreams, unfounded hopes, you would say; and I will not venture to deny it: suspicions to that effect arose too frequently in my own mind. But our wishes are like tinder: the flint and steel of circumstances are continually striking out sparks, which vanish immediately, unless they chance to fall upon the tinder of our wishes; then, they instantly ignite, and the flame of hope is kindled in a moment. (AG., pp. 513–514)

Perhaps it is unkind to lay too much emphasis on Mr. Weston, generally admitted to be one of the least substantial heroes ever to appear in a novel, and we should concentrate on Agnes's own repeated assertions that she is indulging in fancies which may prove to be idle. This pessimism is a good contrast to Rosalie Murray's shallow-brained optimism and to Agnes's sanguine expectations of life at the beginning of the book, and perhaps this is what Anne is really trying to say. She anticipates her father's death, and though the shock is tremendous, she is able to meet it.

It is rather a gloomy doctrine that only by expecting the worst can we hope to get anywhere, and this gloom is reflected in the style which seems, after the heavy satire of the first chapters, to be dull and uninteresting. In *The Tenant of Wildfell Hall* Anne tried her hand at lengthy descriptions of nature and strong touches of realistic debauchery, and these seem overwritten. It may seem harsh to complain that the style of *Agnes Grey* is flat and thin, and that we do not have enough set pieces like the passage describing Agnes's view of her home as she leaves it for the first time or the joyful description of the sea just before Agnes meets Mr. Weston. Even these passages seem a little hackneyed and obvious, with little depth or feeling behind them. As a writer about nature, Anne resembles the eighteenth-century poets more than the Romantics. It is not the voice of Wordsworth, but of Thomson or Goldsmith which we hear behind the following passage:

There was the village spire, and the old grey parsonage beyond it, basking in a slanting beam of sunshine—it was but a sickly ray, but the village and surrounding hills were all in sombre shade, and I hailed the wandering beam as a propitious omen to my home. With clasped hands I fervently implored a blessing on its inhabitants and hastily turned away; for I saw the sunshine was departing; and I carefully avoided another glance, lest I should see it in gloomy shadow, like the rest of the landscape. (AG., p. 367)

With these heavy hints the future of the Grey family is clear, and one reason why such a short work makes such heavy reading is that it is all too often all too clear both what is happening and what is going to happen. It is only when Anne is perhaps not quite certain what she is doing, as when she is describing Agnes's secluded upbringing or her dawning love for Mr. Weston, for which she receives so little encouragement, that the novel appears to have any life in it. It is only when depicting characters who are not totally bad (like Sir Thomas Ashby) or boringly virtuous (like Mr. Weston) that Anne's work has any depth; as a result of the shortness of the book and the concentration on the narrator, this amounts to saying that Rosalie Murray, apart from Agnes herself, is the only interesting character. *The Tenant of Wildfell Hall* has a wider range of characters and in any case is a more interesting work, because in so much of it there is a tension between Anne's obvious purpose and her unconscious achievement.

SIX

The Tenant of Wildfell Hall

The Tenant of Wildfell Hall was published in June 1848, and was presumably written in the two preceding years after Anne had completed work on *Agnes Grey*. If the letter from Newby of February 15th, 1848, found in Emily's desk really concerns *The Tenant of Wildfell Hall*, then Anne was still at work on the novel in 1848. In view of Newby's dilatoriness in publishing *Wuthering Heights* and *Agnes Grey*, and his advice in the letter not to hurry the completion of the novel, it seems unlikely that we do have a reference here to *The Tenant of Wildfell Hall*. Another possible hint at the date of composition is given in the date of June 10th, 1847, at the end of the novel. Anne may have chosen this date at random, but her accuracy about dates in her poems and diary notes makes this unlikely. It would have been possible for her to complete the novel in the summer of 1847 and wait for some time before offering it to the reluctant Newby, who was still concerned with *Wuthering Heights* and *Agnes Grey*. Alternatively, Anne may have spent the latter half of 1847 in making minor revisions to her work.

It would have certainly been possible for *The Tenant of Wildfell Hall* to have been written in a single year from the summer of 1846 to the summer of 1847. *Jane Eyre* was written in very much the same period, and it was a time when Anne appears to have written very little poetry. It is possible, however, that Anne may have been partly drawing upon material she had written in earlier years, and that Helen Huntingdon's narrative, dated from 1841 to 1846, may have been written while she was at Thorp Green.

The episodic character of this long narrative would seem to fit the descriptive title *Passages in the Life of an Individual* better than *Agnes Grey* does.

This uncertainty about the date of composition of *The Tenant of Wildfell Hall* is unfortunate in view of the inevitable association of the story with the events of Anne's own life. Charlotte's statement in the *Biographical Notice of Ellis and Acton Bell* that Anne's mistaken choice of subject was the result of contemplating, "near at hand, and for a long time, the terrible effect of talents misused and faculties abused"[1] gives a strong autobiographical lead. The spectre of Branwell in drunken disgrace forces itself upon us when we consider the story of Arthur Huntingdon's degeneration. Whatever the truth about Branwell's relations with Mrs. Robinson, it is fairly clear that his sisters believed that an adulterous affair had taken place, and adultery, even more than drunkenness, is a feature of *The Tenant of Wildfell Hall*, a feature which brought violent condemnation from prudish contemporary literary reviewers.[2]

Gilbert Markham, a gentleman farmer, describes in the first part of the book how he meets and falls in love with the mysterious Helen Graham, who has recently come with her small son Arthur to live at Wildfell Hall. His love is not encouraged and it receives a sharp blow when scandalmongers suggest that Mrs. Graham is in fact the mistress of Mr. Lawrence, the local squire who owns Wildfell Hall. After hearing Mrs. Graham and Lawrence talking in a compromising fashion, Markham strikes Lawrence, and in order to clear her name and explain why she cannot return Markham's love, Mrs. Graham hands him her account of the previous five years of her life.

This account takes up more than half of the book and reveals how Helen, living with her aunt and uncle, rejects one elderly suitor and against the advice of her aunt marries the dashing Arthur Huntingdon. Fairly soon she sees her mistake, as Arthur's frivolous nature reveals itself, and he either leaves her for long periods to enjoy himself in London or brings back distasteful friends to their home in the country, Grassdale Manor. These friends are Lord Lowborough, who marries Annabella Wilmot, and Arthur Hattersley, who marries Milicent Hargrave; Annabella and Milicent are cousins, and both are Helen's bridesmaids. The narrow circle of Huntingdon's acquaintances is completed by Walter Hargrave, Milicent's brother, and an odious man called Grimsby. Huntingdon flirts with Annabella before and after his marriage, and within three years after the beginning of the narrative Helen discovers that they have been having an affair. By this time Huntingdon has shown himself in his true colours in scenes of drunken debauchery, and we are not surprised that Helen asks Lady Lowborough to leave, and informs Huntingdon that from henceforth she will act merely as his housekeeper. Mr. Hargrave unfortunately seizes the opportunity to press his suit on her, and Helen indignantly rejects this. For two years the Huntingdons continue to live together in mutual hatred, although Huntingdon is often absent. Lord Lowborough discovers his wife's behaviour, Mr. Hargrave continues to plague Helen with his attentions, and finally Huntingdon brings in a new mistress in the disguise of a governess. This prompts Helen to leave with her son for the protection of her brother, who turns out to be Frederick Lawrence; it is not quite clear why Helen's anxiety to prevent herself from being recognised as the wife of Huntingdon also leads her to keep her relationship with her brother a secret.

The narrative then reverts to Gilbert Markham, who apologises to Helen and her brother. Helen reveals that she is in love with Gilbert, but says that they must part, and she does shortly afterwards go back to her husband, who is ill and has nobody to look after him. Huntingdon's illness and death are described in letters from Helen to her brother, and although there are a few false alarms, there are then no obstacles to the final reunion of Gilbert and Helen.

Now it is evident from this bald summary of the plot that though Branwell enters in at several points in the story he cannot simply be equated with Huntingdon. Branwell did not die until after the book was published, and the final scenes of Huntingdon's life must be drawn from Anne's imagination, although she may well have foreseen her brother's death and had worries similar to those of Helen Huntingdon about his chances of salvation. The gradual deterioration of Arthur Huntingdon from the merry scapegrace to the cruel debauchee does seem fairly close to Branwell's decline and fall, although it would be unfair to Branwell to say that he was as intellectually vapid as Huntingdon seems to be even at the beginning of Helen's narrative, or as unpleasant as Huntingdon is shown to be in the final pages. The scenes of drunkenness are usually supposed to be taken from real life, but we should remember that Anne is unlikely to have seen Branwell drunk in company; there is a rather pathetic contrast between Huntingdon's open demand that the butler should bring a bottle of the strongest wine in the cellar and Branwell's feeble and secretive request to John Brown to bring him "Five pence worth of Gin in a proper measure."[3]

Branwell's affair with Mrs. Robinson, real or imagined, is likely to have distressed Anne as much as his drunkenness, and there are various reflections of this affair in the book. Huntingdon's conduct with Lady Lowborough and the governess, Miss Myers, is deplored; Mr. Hargrave's suit is indignantly rejected; Helen reproaches herself, though offering some excuses, for not informing Lord Lowborough earlier of his wife's unfaithfulness; Gilbert Markham is appalled by the scandalous suggestions about Mr. Lawrence and Helen, and when in a moment of high passion he ventures to suggest that the marriage between Helen and Arthur Huntingdon is no proper marriage, both Helen and he himself are horrified by the implications of this Hargrave-like suggestion. It might seem tempting to think that Anne with the example of Branwell raving about Mrs. Robinson before her was trying to say that if you happened to fall in love with someone else's wife, you should behave with great restraint like Gilbert Markham and not give way to your lawless passion like Arthur Huntingdon and Walter Hargrave. But it is difficult to equate the elderly and hardly spotless Mrs. Robinson with Helen Huntingdon, and we must think that Arthur Huntingdon's behaviour with Lady Lowborough and Miss Myers was worse than that of Branwell, who was not himself married and for whom Anne presumably had some residual sympathy.

In addition to autobiographical material as a source for *The Tenant of Wildfell Hall*, we must also be aware of an important literary source. Critics have been aware of the obvious resemblances between *The Tenant of Wildfell Hall* and *Wuthering Heights*;[4] the two houses around which each story is based, the resemblances in initials between Wildfell Hall and Wuthering Heights and between Hargrave, Huntingdon, Hattersley, Hareton, Heathcliff, and Hindley, the gambling, swearing, drinking, and violence that both books have in common, and the fact that each novel has two layers of narrative cannot be coincidence. One explanation would be that Anne was writing very much under her sister's influence, and this might explain why the position of both sisters on certain theological and social questions was fairly similar. But we must not obscure the important differences between the two books, both in what happens and in the authors' attitudes to the main characters. In *Wuthering Heights*, Catherine prefers the conventional Edgar to the violent Heathcliff; her rebellion and that of Heathcliff against this situation is shown without much disapproval on Emily's part through the narrative of Nelly Dean. In *The Tenant of Wildfell Hall*, Gilbert Markham is like Heathcliff in being less aristocratic than his rival, and even has touches of Heathcliff's violence, but he is obviously much more like Edgar Linton in being conventionally, even colourlessly, good, whereas Huntingdon has the satanic attraction of Heathcliff. It sometimes looks as if Anne was taking her sister's book and turning it upside down by making Catherine marry Heathcliff and have her narrate the terrible results. Of course Huntingdon is more timid and contemptible than Heathcliff, but Anne's words in the preface to her second edition of *The Tenant of Wildfell Hall*, "when we have to do with vice and vicious characters, I maintain it is better to depict them as they really are than as they would wish to appear,"[5] suggest a realistic reaction to the romantic extravagances of *Wuthering Heights*.

As in our discussion of *Agnes Grey*, by disposing of the autobiographical element in *The Tenant of Wildfell Hall* we have created a critical difficulty for ourselves. The attitude of Helen Huntingdon to Arthur's levity, drunkenness, and unfaithfulness may bear a rough resemblance to Anne's attitude to Branwell's degeneration, but once we have got over thinking that the one mirrors the other in every respect, we must ask ourselves how far Helen Huntingdon is a factor in Arthur's fall from grace. Biographical critics naturally expect Helen to act as a censorious sister; they forget that Helen is Arthur's wife, that she had been passionately in love with him, and that Arthur's repeated charges that she is partly responsible for his downfall do seem to have a certain amount of right behind them. The skimpy narrative of the first two years of the Huntingdon's marriage, and the fact that we

are, as a result of the episodes at Wildfell Hall, very much on
Helen's side may prevent us from seeing this, but we should not
forget the simple equation that the longer Arthur is married to
Helen the worse his behaviour becomes.

The other main critical difficulty concerns the dual narration.
Whether or not we entirely sympathise with Helen Huntingdon,
her narrative is the most important part of the book, and the
reversion to Gilbert Markham is a bore. Whereas Anne was more
at home in describing the yeomen farmers and clergy in the first
section of the novel than she is in describing aristocratic society in
Helen Huntingdon's narrative,[6] she is much less happy with her
hero than with her heroine. Helen Huntingdon's diary does make
artistic and realistic sense. Anne Brontë's own diary papers show
that a diary filled in at lengthy intervals was nothing extraordinary,
and unlike Anne, Helen has something to say as she narrates the
steps in her gradual disillusion. In contrast, Gilbert Markham's
narrative is extraordinarily clumsy: most editions of the book
obscure the fact that it begins with an address to his brother-in-law
Halford, who marries his sister Rose, and officially takes the form
of long letters to him.[7] But this pretence of an epistolary style is
soon dropped, and this seems just as well, since Markham's
brother-in-law would have to be unusually long-suffering to put up
with these revelations of long-ago events, while Gilbert's frankness and photographic memory seem surprising.

It looks as if Anne is, in these vestiges of an epistolary narrative, hankering after parallels between Gilbert Markham's story
and Helen Huntingdon's. Had Markham chosen as his correspondent not his brother-in-law, whom he presumably did not meet
until long after the events described, but some other friend to
whom he could describe the events as they happened, the story
of his dawning love for Mrs. Graham and gradual disillusion with
the bewitching but shallow Eliza Millward would make sense. As
it is, the praise of Eliza as "charming beyond description, coquettish
without affectation" is extremely awkward, since we later find out
that Eliza is affected, and Gilbert must know this when he
writes.[8] With extreme heavy-handedness Gilbert reminds us of this
when he says that "If I boast of these things now, I shall have to
blush hereafter" (TWH., p. 30). The only excuse for this clumsiness is that Anne is here deliberately drawing attention to the

difference between the diary form and the epistolary form as a means of conveying moral contrition.

One obvious function of the first section of the book is to arouse pity for Helen Huntingdon. Poor, lonely, and oppressed by the malicious tittle-tattle of the neighbourhood, she is in the romantic situation of Wildfell Hall an obvious target for our sympathy and affection. Her reserve and her coldness are later explained by the difficulties of her situation, and even her rather unattractive dogmatism about the necessity of making her son loathe strong drink enables us to see her conduct in the middle section of the book in a more attractive light.

Like *Agnes Grey*, *The Tenant of Wildfell Hall* appears at first sight to be a rather awkwardly constructed moralising work full of black-and-white oppositions. Some of the awkwardness is removed and some of the moralising softened if we regard *The Tenant of Wildfell Hall* as a novel stressing the importance of experience. This kind of emphasis is made clear in the passage where Helen justifies her rather peculiar recommendation of aversion-therapy to alcohol for Arthur. Mrs. Markham says that this will make a milksop of him, and Gilbert says that a boy must not be brought up in a hothouse atmosphere. Helen asks pointedly whether girls should be brought up in a hothouse atmosphere, and then in a telling speech, to which Gilbert can only rather feebly reply that ladies must always have the last word, makes a bold plea for both sexes being educated in the same way:

"You would have us encourage our sons to prove all things by their own experience, while our daughters must not even profit by the experience of others. Now I would have both so benefit by the experience of others, and the precepts of a higher authority, that they should know beforehand to refuse the evil and choose the good, and require no experimental proofs to teach them the evil of transgression." (TWH., p. 26)

With this fine feminist plea in mind we can perhaps look at the main section of the novel in a fresh light. Helen Huntingdon as the embodiment of purity and righteousness is an unattractive figure: we can sympathise with her more easily if we regard her instead as one of those hothouse plants, sent out into the world unarmed against her foes, and ignorant of the snares that beset her path. Of course it could be argued that Helen is not so unarmed: her aunt does explicitly warn her against the superficial attractions of Huntingdon, but perhaps Helen's aunt's conduct is to be blamed, not because she guards Helen too little, but because she guards her too much, and certainly by pressing the claims of the totally unattractive Mr. Boarham she succeeds in driving Helen into the arms of his younger rival.

Mr. Boarham, and the even more odious Mr. Wilmot, together with the jealousy aroused by Annabella Wilmot, are all factors in explaining why Helen falls so hopelessly in love with Arthur. The marriage is a mistake, and yet we feel it is not necessarily doomed. What could Helen have done to save it? The answer presumably is that she could have been more aware of what Huntingdon was doing, and less gentle and forgiving to him at an early stage in the marriage.

This may seem an odd conclusion in view of the fact that Milicent Hargrave, who is several times held up as a contrast to Helen by reason of her gentleness, does succeed in saving her marriage to the brutal Ralph Hattersley, who lacks Huntingdon's redeeming graces. It would seem that gentleness pays, since Hattersley ends the novel as a reformed character, but the two cases are not really similar, as Milicent enters her marriage with few illusions, and Huntingdon's example, backed up by a fierce speech of Helen's listing Milicent's complaints, is a potent factor in Hattersley's redemption. Similar warnings early in the Huntingdon marriage might have saved the day, but Helen is still too much under the spell of her early illusions to do anything but offer gentleness to Huntingdon after his first return from London.

Helen's first major quarrel with her husband occurs before they leave for London, and is sparked off by her husband's account of his scandalous affair with a married woman. On this occasion we are not very sympathetic to Helen's stern and priggish attitude, but it does succeed in bringing about a temporary reconciliation, and we are presumably meant to contrast this sternness with later efforts at appeasement. Helen is perhaps too mild when she discovers Arthur holding hands with Lady Lowborough and when, after several heavy warnings which she disregards, she discovers Arthur and Lady Lowborough are having an affair, it is far too late.

Of course Anne's attitude to the Huntingdon marriage is the

essentially ambivalent one we must take to all bad marriages: while with the one hand she is pointing out where the marriage went wrong, with the other she is saying that it should never have taken place. This latter theme is certainly brought out in the parallel story of Lord Lowborough, whose second wife is so surprisingly a success, of Esther Hargrave, who is nearly bullied by her mother into marrying someone quite unsuitable, and of Frederick Lawrence, whose "inexperience" nearly makes him the victim of the unattractive Jane Wilson. One person who does not really look before he leaps (Anne twice uses this hackneyed phrase) is Gilbert Markham, who wishes to marry Helen Huntingdon because he falls in love with her and continues to pursue her against the advice of his friends and relatives, just as Helen had pursued Arthur. Of course the advice of Gilbert's friends is wrong, whereas that of Helen's aunt is right, and a great deal of stress is laid on Helen and Gilbert's common intellectual tastes, but Gilbert's wild jealousy at the thought that Helen may be Lawrence's mistress shows that it is not just her love of *Marmion* that makes Helen so attractive.

Perhaps it is in order to reinforce the message that it is wiser to look before you leap that the courtship of Helen and Gilbert encounters such difficulties. It is never really explained why Helen goes back to her husband, nor when he is dead why both parties are so shy about renewing their acquaintance. Frederick Lawrence, preoccupied with his own courtship and perhaps bearing a grudge against Gilbert for hitting him over the head, makes an unsatisfactory intermediary, but the idea that Helen's social superiority is the main obstacle to the match does not ring true, as Gilbert has only to meet Helen for the barrier to be removed.

The concluding section of the narrative is, apart from Helen's letters, disappointing.[9] We miss the dissection of a marriage that is so prominent in Helen's journal, and the mystery of who Helen is in the opening part of the story has been cleared up. The convenient tidying-up of loose ends, relating the lives of the minor characters, is clumsy, and the rewarding of good people like Mary Millward and Esther Hargrave and the punishment of bad people like Mr. Hargrave and Jane Wilson is schematic and obvious. We cannot help feeling that Anne has forsaken realism at this point in order to drive her moral lesson home. The removal of Huntingdon, unlike the parallel removal of Mrs. Rochester, seems too convenient to be true, and this is because Gilbert Markham is a character much less sympathetic than Jane Eyre. Of course the death of Huntingdon is related by Helen, who like Mr. Rochester tries to save her evil spouse from death, nearly killing herself in the process, but we hear nothing of her feelings about the possibility of marrying again; she seems more concerned with the fate of her husband's soul. Theology does not appear to be an interest which Gilbert and Helen share, and Gilbert is prepared to speculate on the possibility of marrying again, although for a man previously so impetuous he is now rather hesitant about pressing his suit. The experiment of combining the two narrators in the final section of the book is not a success: Anne seems unable to shift focus sufficiently quickly and Gilbert seems as a result to have inherited some of Helen's feminine reserve; it is almost the case that it is actually she who proposes marriage.

Contemporary critics almost unanimously found fault with *The Tenant of Wildfell Hall* on account of its coarseness; modern admirers of Anne Brontë have praised her frankness about sexual matters and her realistic description of scenes of violence.[10] Neither verdict seems wholly accurate. So far as sexual explicitness is concerned, the novel is remarkably reticent. It is simply not true that the slamming of the bedroom door in Huntingdon's face reverberates through the novel;[11] the scene where Helen tells her husband that henceforth she will be a wife in name only is written with quiet tact, but thereafter we are not told about either party's feelings. It is not made clear why Helen is more annoyed by Arthur's adultery with Miss Myers than by his affair with Lady Lowborough. In the early part of the marriage sex is conspicuous for its absence, though it is hinted that Arthur amuses himself with other women while he is in London, as he had before his marriage, much to Helen's indignation. One wonders if Anne Brontë was aware of the implications of Helen's pregnancy; certainly she makes nothing of the fact that Arthur excusably sends Helen away from London when she is pregnant, and less excusably leaves her in the country for a long time.

The scenes of violence on the other hand are painfully detailed, and here, as occasionally in *Wuthering Heights*, what is obviously meant to be shocking fails to shock, because it almost seems comic. The drunken horseplay of Huntingdon and his friends does not seem as appalling as Helen and her creator would like us to think. Victorian readers would be very shocked by such behaviour in front of ladies, but one is left wondering how much the lady who described these scenes knew about male conviviality. Much more effective than the detailed description of the drunken party is the damning sentence at the end when Grimsby and Hattersley bring Huntingdon up to bed: "He himself was no longer laughing now, but sick and stupid. I will write no more about that" (TWH., p. 281). There is a similar contrast between the forced and slightly artificial description of Huntingdon's death, and the telling comment after he is dead, that the coffin must be closed as soon as possible. The evil-smelling reality of a Victorian death-bed is shown much better by this brief statement than by all Helen and Arthur's previous protestations.

In general Anne fails to convince us in her purple patches. The scenes of violence, Markham's account of his jealousy, Helen's religious sermons, and even the set pieces describing the natural scenery conforming to the mood of the principal character, all make embarrassing reading. We can see Anne making a conscious effort to impress us, and we are not impressed; indeed like Charlotte we feel sometimes that the choice of subject is an entire mistake. A very good example of the lady protesting too much occurs when Helen reflects in the first summer of her marriage how much she misses her husband, and how she wishes she could share the joys of summer with him. The passage is overwritten, and though in its best parts it reminds us of the oppressive but attractive descriptions of summer in Thomson's *Seasons*, at its worst it is a reminder of some of the extravagances of Charlotte's or Branwell's juvenilia. Nevertheless it could stand as an acceptable part of the novel, with its undertones of heavy languor, reminding us of Helen's pregnancy, and calm before the coming storm, as an indication of the state of the Huntingdon marriage, were it not for the shrill and insistent reminders that Arthur is in the wrong during this scene "because he cannot feel its freshening influence" (TWH., p. 228).

By insisting that Arthur is in the wrong, Anne narrows the scope of her novel. She could, and indeed at times does, write a fine account of a marriage that fails, and on a broader plane, of the failures of innocence and inexperience. Obviously even this theme for her novel is more limited and less profound than the cosmic gropings of Emily or Charlotte, and it is perhaps in an attempt to rival her sisters that Anne resorts to her purple patches in order to bridge the gap. These attempts are disastrous, but the achievement in spite of them is not so small as to merit complete disdain.

SEVEN

The Professor

The manuscript of *The Professor* is dated June 27th, 1846, and this is presumably the date when Charlotte completed the novel. It then went to six publishers, who curtly refused it, until in August 1847, Charlotte received a much more courteous refusal from Smith, Elder and Co., expressing interest in a three-volume novel. Charlotte sent them *Jane Eyre*, but after its success still contemplated recasting *The Professor* and turning it into a three-volume work. In December 1847 she wrote to W. S. Williams about this possibility, but her publishers evidently discouraged this, and instead she began *Shirley*. In February 1851 she wrote to George Smith after trying for the ninth time to get *The Professor* published in something like its original form; evidently Smith, although not giving an outright refusal, had urged her to try something new. Charlotte said that she would lock up *The Professor* "by himself in a cupboard," and embarked upon *Villette*, which, since it contained some of the same materials as *The Professor*, would seem to have put an end to the possibility of the latter ever being published. On Charlotte's death Smith saw the merits of publishing a posthumous novel. Sir James Kay Shuttleworth was eager to edit *The Professor*, but Mrs. Gaskell, after refusing the task herself, said that it should be entrusted to Mr. Nicholls. He made a few alterations, through which in some cases it is possible to re-create Charlotte's original version. Charlotte's own corrections, made probably after the publication of *Shirley* when she wrote a new preface for the novel, can also be traced in the manuscript.[1]

Both Kay Shuttleworth and Mrs. Gaskell found in *The Professor* traces of moral coarseness, and some of Mr. Nicholls's alterations appear to have been motivated by a desire to expunge this. What principally worried Mrs. Gaskell, however, were reminders of the Heger story, and though initially relieved at the dissimilarities between *The Professor* and Charlotte's own experiences in Belgium, she was still anxious about its publication, wishing that Mr. Nicholls had altered more and thinking that the novel in its original version might make Charlotte misunderstood. In the event, *The Professor* was not attacked for coarseness, and Mrs. Gaskell's own tactful handling of the Heger story in her biography ensured that for many years the autobiographical element in *The Professor* received little attention. With the publication of Charlotte's letters to Monsieur Heger the situation was altered. Both *The Professor* and *Villette* contain as their chief element a love affair in Belgium between a pupil-teacher and a schoolmaster, with the proprietress of the school in which the action takes place playing a sinister part as she tries for selfish reasons to separate the lovers. It is very easy to make Charlotte into the original of Lucy Snowe and Frances Henri, Monsieur Heger into the original of Paul Emanuel and William Crimsworth, while both Madame Beck and Mademoiselle Reuter stand for Madame Heger.

But these crude equations obviously will not work. William Crimsworth is not at all like Paul Emanuel, being in many respects much more like Lucy Snowe, who in turn lacks Frances Henri's air of gentle submissiveness. The equation between Madame Beck and Mademoiselle Reuter is a little more convincing; their slyness, their success in managing their schools, and their efforts to keep the lovers apart are very similar, and inevitably remind us of Madame Heger. Mrs. Gaskell when she first read *The Professor* saw the description of Mademoiselle Reuter as its most dangerous feature, although she comforted herself that Mademoiselle Reuter played a comparatively minor role in the novel.[2] Even in this minor role, however, there are marked differences between Mademoiselle Reuter on the one hand and Madame Beck and Madame Heger on the other. The latter are or have been married, and as good wives and mothers seem to have solid virtues which the flirtatious Mademoiselle Reuter lacks. Indeed one of the odd features of *The Professor* is the strong emphasis placed upon the amount of sexual attraction between Mademoiselle Reuter and Crimsworth. Nor is there any equivalent in *Villette* or in real life for the character of Monsieur Pelet. It has been argued that Charlotte was inspired by her feelings towards Mrs. Robinson in portraying Mademoiselle Reuter's laxity of morals.[3]

Faced by these difficulties, students of *The Professor* have tended to say that differences between it and Charlotte's own story spring from Charlotte's wish to disguise her own experiences, as the wounds from these were still too fresh.[4] Hence *Villette* with its description of such real-life incidents as the visit to the confessional, and with events seen from the eyes of a woman, is regarded as more autobiographical, and since it is a much greater novel, the biographical school of criticism seems to be able to turn *The Professor* to its own advantage, maintaining that the faults of *The Professor* arise from Charlotte's inability to write outside her own experience.

As we shall see, it is naive to think of *Villette* as a simple autobiographical novel, and it is also naive to regard *The Professor* as autobiography clumsily disguised. If Charlotte had wanted to cover her own tracks she would have been well advised to be more discreet in her topographical references: as it is, Belgium, Brussels, and the locality of the pensionnat Heger appear without any disguise, and Mademoiselle Zoraïde Reuter's Christian name has the same initial letter as that of Madame Zoë Heger. Where the disguise appears to come in is in the two main weaknesses of the novel, the scenes before Crimsworth goes to Belgium, and the male narrator.

The novel opens with a clumsy piece of narrative technique; William Crimsworth is writing a letter to an old school friend of his about what happened after he had left Eton. As it turns out, the friend never gets the letter, and Crimsworth continues the narrative for his own amusement. In it he describes how he rejected the patronage of his aristocratic maternal uncles, and tried to seek employment with his brother Edward, who, like his father, was an industrial magnate. Edward treated William with harshness and neglect, and eventually William, thanks to the interference of a neighbouring industrialist called Hunsden, resigns his menial post and goes to Belgium. Hunsden introduces him to a Mr. Brown, who finds him a post as a teacher at the school of

Monsieur Pelet. Here Crimsworth triumphs as a teacher and succeeds in winning the favour of Monsieur Pelet and attracting the attention of Mademoiselle Reuter, the proprietress of the neighbouring girls' school. Invited to teach at this school, Crimsworth with a little more difficulty achieves a similar success. For a time he thinks about the possibility of a love affair between himself and Mademoiselle Reuter, but is soon disillusioned when he overhears a conversation between his two employers, who are engaged to be married. Crimsworth does not seem unduly disturbed by this; he is more angered by the lack of principle shown by Monsieur Pelet and Mademoiselle Reuter than by any feelings of jealousy, and in any case he soon starts falling rather rapidly in love with a pupil-teacher at Mademoiselle Reuter's school, Frances Henri Evans. Mademoiselle Reuter in spite of her engagement is still attracted by Crimsworth and dismisses Frances Henri, refusing to disclose her whereabouts. Crimsworth searches for her and finds her; now the only obstacle to their marrying is that they have no money, since Crimsworth is unwilling to serve either Monsieur Pelet or Mademoiselle Reuter. Fortunately, he has rescued a boy from drowning, and thanks to the recommendation of his father is able to get another job. Hunsden arrives from England expecting to find Crimsworth married to Mademoiselle Reuter, but he is soon put right when he is introduced to Frances Henri, to whom after some snobbish doubts he gives a grudging approval. Crimsworth and Frances Henri marry, and the novel ends with a rapid summary of the unromantic way they lived happily ever after: Crimsworth succeeds in his profession, Frances Henri starts a school of her own, and they have a son.

The two principal themes of the book would seem to be the importance of a man's earning his living by his own exertions and the importance of choosing a wife with a good character who shares tastes in preference to one with more sensual or material attractions. It is thus difficult to agree with those who wish to say that Crimsworth is Charlotte Brontë in disguise, and that she is showing through his story her own desire to succeed as a teacher by her efforts. We do know that Charlotte had ideas about careers for women, and that what Frances Henri and Lucy Snowe achieve, a school of their own, was also her ambition. But the ways in which Frances Henri and Lucy Snowe achieve their success, with male financial support and encouragement, are quite different from Crimsworth's painstaking efforts. Charlotte may be saying that women should have equal opportunities with men to earn a competency by their own endeavours, although she hardly stresses this feminist view against the conventional view that a woman's proper goal is a husband and family. What she cannot be saying is that women do have equal opportunities; Crimsworth succeeds, and Frances Henri fails as an assistant teacher, because Crimsworth impresses pupils and staff by his masculinity.

Similarly Charlotte may have thought that the affinity between herself and Monsieur Heger was a moral and intellectual one, whereas Madame Heger was linked to her husband by material and sensual ties. If she did think this she probably deceived herself about her own situation and about the nature of love, which she portrayed with much more vigour in *Jane Eyre*. But the auto-biographical element in *The Professor* then appears in a most peculiar form: it is no longer Charlotte who is Crimsworth, but Monsieur Heger, disguised improbably as an Englishman and given all kinds of thoughts and feelings which Charlotte would have considered impertinent to ascribe to her beloved master.

It seems safest to bypass the autobiographical hazards in *The Professor*, but if we do so we find ourselves in critical difficulties. The early part of the novel, which when she revised it Charlotte admitted was very weak,[5] is explicable if we imagine Charlotte wishing to write about her lonely lot, but lacking the courage and the imagination to present that portrait of a friendless woman which she was so successfully to create in writing *Villette*. The male narrator is a suitable disguise for the rawness of Charlotte's feelings in the first section of the book and the fact that he is English is a mask for his resemblance to Monsieur Heger in the second half of the book. The metamorphosis from the unsuccessful clerk of the first few chapters, meekly submitting to the menial role that his brother allots him, to the successful schoolmaster in Belgium, impressing all and sundry by his forceful personality, can be explained if we assume that Charlotte is making Crimsworth stand for herself originally and then, while she takes the role of Frances Henri, Crimsworth becomes Monsieur Heger. If we cannot make this assumption, we are compelled to ask why Charlotte, who wrote so well about independence, loneliness, and woman's lot in *Villette*, should have in treating the same themes in *The Professor* saddled herself with the difficulties of an unnecessary introduction in England, and a male narrator whose character changes when he leaves England.

These are real difficulties. Unlike the opening chapters of *Villette* and *Jane Eyre*, set in a different milieu from the main story but containing characters whom we are to meet again, *The Professor*'s opening chapters introduce us only to Hunsden, who, as Mrs. Humphry Ward pointed out,[6] is a thoroughly unsatisfactory character, promising much but achieving little. Whereas the opening chapters of *Jane Eyre* and *Villette* give a wonderfully complete portrait of the two heroines of the book, whose characters, consistent throughout, give unity to the whole novel, Crimsworth is colourless, and his character changes once he leaves England. Unlike Jane Austen, Charlotte Brontë was not shy about entering the field of masculine conversation, but inevitably with a masculine narrator this conversation looms large and rings false. The feminine introspection, the tepid sexuality, and the jocular jousts with Hunsden are further consequences of the masculine narrator, and it is very tempting to look to Monsieur Heger as a means of saving Charlotte's literary reputation.

The need to disguise the presence of Monsieur Heger cannot, however, excuse two irritating faults in *The Professor*, Charlotte's frequent lapses into French, and her frequent reminders that her narrator is at liberty to organise his narrative in any way she wishes.[7] The French dialogue seems as artificial as the way in which foreign characters in films speak to each other in broken English, and it appears to serve no useful purpose except in the conversations between Crimsworth and Frances Henri. Here Crimsworth's insistence that Frances Henri should speak in English seems to show him in an unpleasantly didactic role, while Frances Henri is a more attractive mixture of dutiful obedience and impulsive disobedience. When Crimsworth proposes to Frances he allows her to speak French for a time, and she says she is to him "Votre dévouée élève, qui vous aime de tout son coeur." Then he asks, "Will my pupil consent to pass her life with me? Speak English now, Frances" (P., p. 229), and obediently, if slowly, Frances accepts. Perhaps this change of tongues is meant to symbolise the change from pupil to wife, but we cannot help feeling that it shows that the pedant in Crimsworth is stronger than the lover, and we are glad that Frances, impervious to the strong doses of Wordsworth that Crimsworth administers, continues to speak French after her marriage. In earlier scenes of the book, although Crimsworth says that he is not absolutely confident about his accent he is less reluctant to conduct a conversation in French with his pupils; they are presumably less proficient than Frances, less intimate with him, and their French perhaps does show up the awkwardness of Crimsworth's position in a foreign land. The same could be said of the conversations in French with Mademoiselle Reuter and Monsieur Pelet, but here the constant interchange between French and English is very awkward, and like many attempts at realism only seems to remind us how unrealistic it is to find Monsieur Pelet and Mademoiselle Reuter speaking such admirable English.

The French dialogues are an irritating but hardly fundamental fault; monoglot readers can safely skip them without missing much. More disturbing are the tricks that Crimsworth plays with us as narrator. In Chapter 12 Crimsworth sketches for us the various inmates of Mademoiselle Reuter's school. He begins with a portrait of three vicious girls, even more deplorable characters than the three badly behaved girls who had disturbed his first lesson. There are then brief descriptions of poor Sylvie, tormented by religion, the English pupils bad and good, three teachers, Zéphyrine, Pélagie, and Suzette, and then "a fourth maîtresse I sometimes saw. . . . her name, I think, was Mdlle. Henri." There follows a paragraph of praise for Mademoiselle Reuter, "the sensible, sagacious, affable directress" (P., p. 105).

Now it is no doubt right that Crimsworth, involved in the school and encaptured by the siren charms of its directress, should in his pedagogical division of the establishment into categories and examples mention his future wife almost as an afterthought and be uncertain of her name. We feel it is slightly sly and dishonest of Crimsworth not to make more of Mademoiselle Henri on her first appearance, just as we feel it dishonest of Lucy Snowe not to reveal that the stranger who presented her with violets is Paul Emanuel until we are three-quarters of the way through the book, but one of the major differences between *Jane Eyre* on the one hand and *Villette* and *The Professor* on the other is that the narrators of the latter are essentially untrustworthy. What is unforgiveable is the clumsiness of "her name, I think, was Mdlle. Henri." Presumably at the time of writing Crimsworth had not forgotten his wife's maiden name.

The clue to this apparent forgetfulness is the device with which the novel opens. Crimsworth is writing to an old school friend. He closes his letter at the point when he is staying his first and only night at Crimsworth Hall. Charlotte is obviously not happy with the epistolary technique; as Sheridan does in *The Critic* she makes Crimsworth inform his correspondent of facts he knows already:

I wrote instantly to Edward—you know Edward—my only brother, ten years my senior, married to a rich mill-owner's daughter, and now possessor of the mill and business which was my father's before he failed. You are aware that my father—once reckoned a Croesus of wealth—became bankrupt a short time previous to his death. (P., p. 7)

The opening twelve pages of the manuscript of *The Professor* appear to have been written at a time different from the rest of the novel, and we cannot really blame Charlotte for this particular false start.[8] A brave effort has been made by one of the few modern critics of *The Professor* prepared to take it seriously to show that the beginning and end of the novel, which show Crimsworth secure in his competency and happily married, are deliberately set against the bulk of the novel in which the raw and callow Crimsworth sets down his experiences without reflection as they occur.[9] The contrast between *now* and *then*, the time Crimsworth wrote about his experiences and the time he suffers them, is stressed at various points in the novel, and it is presumably right that this point should be stressed in a book which aims to show its hero growing into mature independence as a result of his own efforts. What is wrong is the intrusion of the presumably mature Crimsworth at various points in the novel to remind the reader in a fairly immature manner that he is in the narrator's hands. Jane Eyre and Lucy Snowe are both more subtle and more effective in their use of the contrast between past and present.

Criticism of the early chapters of the book and of Crimsworth's unattractive traits do seem less valid if we regard the book as one like *Jane Eyre* and for that matter *Agnes Grey*, in which the narrator looks back over his past mistakes and shows how he profited from their lesson. Crimsworth is a pitiful creature at the beginning of the novel and is perhaps unduly complacent at the end, but at any rate *The Professor* traces some pattern of spiritual growth. What he learns in his stay at X—— is independence: the experiment of semi-independence as an employee of his brother is a failure, just as the almost total dependence that he would have experienced at the hands of his maternal relatives would have been a failure. It is through the agency of Hunsden that Crimsworth manages to break free from the influence of his brother, and it is through Hunsden's much less oppressive patronage that he contrives to secure the job in Brussels.

At X—— Crimsworth is a subservient clerk whose only respite from work in the counting house and sitting quietly in his lodgings is the invitation to his brother's dance, where he is a sad wallflower. In Brussels he quickly secures employment, soon establishes his authority in his first school, finds himself an additional job at the girls' school, where again he is an instant success, and imagines himself, apparently with some justification, to be something of a lady-killer. The change is a sudden one, and the personality of Hunsden is insufficiently developed for us to be able to explain the metamorphosis simply as a result of his influence. Though Hunsden's patronage is more indirect and less obnoxious than that provided by Crimsworth's relatives it remains true that Crimsworth has hardly obtained complete independence sufficient to justify his newly won self-confidence.

In *Jane Eyre* it is fairly easy to see the heroine winning her way through to a compromise between selfish passion and chilling selflessness after being tempted to give way to either extreme. It is possible that Hunsden is meant to stand for a similar extreme, and that Crimsworth's sudden change to self-assertion is a result of his falling under his friend's spell, in the same way that Jane Eyre by following the example of Helen Burns and Miss Temple is in danger of losing her individuality. It is difficult, however, to see exactly what Hunsden is standing for; *The Professor* is so full of weighty abstractions like Reason and Passion, and Hunsden with his hatred of aristocrats and pride in his family name is such a mass of contradictions, that it is hard to say in what direction he is pushing William Crimsworth.

Hunsden is hostile to Crimsworth's brother and to the Seacombe connection. In urging and helping Crimsworth to make a new start in Brussels he obviously is telling him to break away from his family connections, and for a time Crimsworth does just this. Yet family ties still do have some meaning, as is shown by Crimsworth's anxiety about the fate of his mother's portrait; Hunsden's contempt about this sentimentality shows that he believes in theory one should break away from one's family, although his practical kindness in rescuing the portrait and presenting it to Crimsworth indicates that in this matter, as in others, he does not always live up to his beliefs.

Much more important than Crimsworth's mother is Crimsworth's wife. In X—— Crimsworth is weary and solitary, and Hunsden is the dashing star of the ballroom, cutting out Sam Waddy in the dance, and causing a stir among match-making mothers and their darling daughters. It is not that Crimsworth is not interested in women: on the contrary he shows an unbrotherly interest in his brother's wife, and at the dance he would "have liked well enough to be introduced to some pleasing and intelligent girl, and to have freedom and opportunity to show that I could both feel and communicate the pleasure of social intercourse" (P., p. 24). But he is too shy, too conscious of his social inferiority to have any success with women, whereas in Belgium, under Hunsden's influence and freed from the restraints of his English upbringing, Crimsworth imagines that all sorts of women are falling in love with him, and in many cases it turns out that he is right.

Charlotte's choice of a male narrator has been generally regarded as a mistake. Crimsworth's introspection about the impression that he is creating seems a feminine intrusion, and the impression he does create seems a pale hangover from the Byronic extravagances of Angrian heroes. Yet it is not impossible to imagine a shy intellectual when emancipated from the shackles of English decorum and the English class system imagining that women of all ages on the supposedly immoral continent are ready to fall in love with him, and, since Crimsworth is not unattractive, once he thinks it likely that Mademoiselle Reuter and some of his pupils will love him, it is not impossible for them actually to do so. Crimsworth's speculations about Madame Reuter, Zoraïde's mother, and his un-academic interest in some of his more handsome pupils seem unattractive traits, but they are not unrealistic. Nor of course does Charlotte mean us to think that this side of Crimsworth is attrac-tive. In spite of the Angrian precedents Crimsworth's doggish preoccupation with the physical charms of his pupils and Made-moiselle Reuter is not meant to be admired. We are not meant to approve of this behaviour any more than we are meant to admire Crimsworth's shyness when working for his brother; indeed the parallels between Mrs. Edward Crimsworth and Mademoiselle Reuter when she becomes Madame Pelet are obvious. This change from hopeful shyness to prudent boldness is the result of Huns-den's influence; Hunsden, as is made clear when he comes to Belgium, thinks in theory of women rationally either as animals or as good social connections. He thinks that Crimsworth is about to marry Mademoiselle Reuter, and is quite prepared to believe, after he has learnt of the Pelet marriage, that Crimsworth is having an affair with Madame Pelet: the more idealistic side of him is shocked by the thought of the affairs, and we see the contradic-tory nature of Hunsden in the account at the end of the book of his failure to find the right wife.

Crimsworth does find the right wife, one who suits his nature, in Frances Henri. Hunsden, although he comes to admire Frances Henri, is with the rationalist side of him shocked by Frances Henri's lack of connections and beauty. It is because she lacks these qualities that Crimsworth does not at first recognise her existence in the passage where so clumsily he pretends not to know her name. At the time his main interest is Mademoiselle Reuter, a good connection, with a certain amount of physical attraction; later reference to Madame Pelet weighing twelve stone and earlier references to her being a dumpy woman should not be taken as belittling her sexual charms, as running through all Charlotte's novels we find an equation between ample proportions and un-worthy sensual allurements.[10]

Charlotte's unusual frankness about the nature of Mademoiselle Reuter's attractiveness is slightly weakened by the fact that Crims-worth is not so frank. Just before he overhears Monsieur Pelet and Mademoiselle Reuter talking in the garden he runs over the features that would make her a good wife.

"She is a fascinating little woman," I continued in voiceless soliloquy; "her image forms a pleasant picture in memory; I know she is not what the world calls pretty—no matter, there is harmony in her aspect, and I like it; her brown hair, her blue eye, the freshness of her cheek, the whiteness of her neck, all suit my taste." (P., p. 109)

He then goes on to say that he cannot bear the thought of marrying "a pretty doll, a fair fool," and that Zoraïde's intelligence is a factor in her favour. Her honesty is more open to question, but he is prepared to give him the benefit of the doubt, until at that very moment her perfidy is revealed in talking to Monsieur Pelet. Crimsworth spends a sleepless night, but then philosophically consoles himself with the thought that "physically Zoraïde might have suited me but . . . our souls were not in harmony" (P., p. 114).

One is inclined to think that Crimsworth is initially deceiving himself when he rates Zoraïde's looks so low, and that he underestimates the extent of his jealousy. This impression is confirmed in the chapter when after acknowledging his love for Frances Henri, Crimsworth explains how Mademoiselle Reuter was in love with him, how he felt both gratification and degradation "in receiving this luscious incense from an attractive and still young worshipper" (P., p. 189), and how he felt obliged to leave the Pelet household for fear that "a practical modern French novel would be in full process of concoction under the roof of the unsuspecting Pelet" (P., p. 192).

Crimsworth's reluctance to press his suit with the engaging and willing Frances Henri is difficult to explain, but not inexplicable. After he has found her in the cemetery he says, "I loved her as she stood there, penniless and parentless; for a sensualist charmless, for me a treasure" (P., p. 173). But, as he will acknowledge later when he says, "It appeared, then, that I too was a sensualist, in my temperate and fastidious way" (P., p. 233), Crimsworth is not as aloof from physical charms as he thinks; this we discover in the intervening chapter when he finds it so hard to resist Mademoiselle Reuter's advances. He also is not so swept away by

Frances Henri as to ignore the need to earn a living, and the practical steps he has to take in order to gain a competency occupy his attention when he is not warding off Mademoiselle Reuter. Having gained his freedom from the Pelet household and obtained a new post, Crimsworth, one would have thought, could have married Frances Henri straightaway, especially as she expresses her love for him so blatantly, but after she has accepted his proposal, he falls a victim to hypochondria.

This hypochondria has baffled commentators. It has been connected with sexual guilt.[11] It seems more probable that at this stage Crimsworth, still partly under Hunsden's influence owing to the sudden arrival of his friend in Belgium, finds Frances insufficiently endowed with sensual and material attractions. In his slightly tepid account of her he does say, "she was not handsome, she was not rich, she was not even accomplished" (P., p. 232). Crimsworth overcomes his hypochondria, Frances overcomes Hunsden in debate, and, though the account of the Crimsworths' married life is a little hurried with too much emphasis on money rather than love, we can believe that the novel has reached a satisfactory conclusion, especially as the slightly insipid Frances does show herself a character of some mettle in the final chapters, first in her spirited replies to Hunsden, then as headmistress of a successful school, and finally as a mother. As with so many of Charlotte's novels, the last word is given not to the Crimsworths, but to Charlotte's other successful creation, Mademoiselle Reuter, now Madame Pelet, a useful reminder of the bad choice Crimsworth nearly made.

Charlotte's exploration of Crimsworth's state of mind is interesting and original, but the tendency to lapse into abstractions and the peculiar narrative method are more than enough to put off most readers. W. S. Williams deserves great credit for seeing that the kind of talent which Charlotte displayed in The Professor could be developed in further novels. She used her Brussels material again in Villette, but in all three later novels she showed innocence developing into maturity through experience, she contrasted the past with the present more subtly than in The Professor, and she explored variations on the theme of one person in love with two people. Her later novels are longer, and involve more characters; there is less need for abstract soliloquy, although Charlotte or her narrator still soliloquises, and less excuse for seeing the novels as a series of disconnected episodes, although Charlotte is still accused of this fault. The plain and penniless Frances Henri gains even more of our sympathy when she becomes the centre of the story in later novels, and shorn of his feminine traits Crimsworth emerges as Charlotte's more convincing if still slightly preposterous heroes in her main novels. In other words, unlike the juvenilia, *The Professor* is a real mine of information for Charlotte's major works; her faults are even more obvious, and the excuses for these faults slightly less convincing, but if we are prepared to admit these excuses, we are in the properly charitable frame of mind for *Jane Eyre* and *Villette*.

By the time she wrote *Jane Eyre* and *Villette*, Charlotte had softened slightly. Her passionate desire for realism, which she announced in her preface, found expression in less dreary forms than the sham epistolary narrative, the lifeless account of industrial life, the flat Flemish landscape, the schoolgirl French, the pretence at love without sex, the sudden threatened lapse into sex without love, and the boring authorial intrusions which make *The Professor* such a drab novel. After the triumph of *Jane Eyre*, Charlotte was prepared to say that the middle and latter portions of *The Professor* contained "more pith, more substance, more reality" than much of her first published novel.[12] While making due allowance for the special pleading which an author can be permitted when writing in favour of a first novel intended for publication, one can only say in this instance that Charlotte is in certain ways as much of a hypocrite as William Crimsworth.

EIGHT

Jane Eyre

The reputation of *Jane Eyre* has fluctuated almost as widely as the fortunes of Jane herself. The initial success of the book was obvious, although there were some reservations from Lady East-lake and others who found the book coarse. These reservations were hard to sustain after Charlotte's death, and with the publication of Charlotte's story by Mrs. Gaskell, this her first published novel, to which Mrs. Gaskell paid a great deal of attention, was accepted by the Victorian public as a masterpiece. At the end of the nineteenth century Mrs. Humphry Ward in her prefaces to the Haworth edition of the Brontë novels pointed out some of the obvious faults of Charlotte's book, which she found inferior to *Wuthering Heights*; and in the reaction to Victorian taste which set in at the beginning of the twentieth century it was natural that *Jane Eyre*, a Victorian classic, should lose ground at the expense of Emily's novel, which the Victorians found hard to comprehend. The nadir in Charlotte Brontë's reputation came when F. R. Leavis said that critically speaking there was only one Brontë, although David Cecil had come fairly close to saying the same thing when he praised *Jane Eyre* with some fairly loud damns. Recently there has been more critical interest in Charlotte as a novelist. Some studies of her imagery and symbolism, in articles which explored, perhaps a little fancifully at times, new aspects of the meaning of *Jane Eyre* not understood by earlier critics, were followed by several full-length books which reasserted Charlotte's claim to greatness in her first published novel by drawing on these and similar explorations.[1]

Thus the wheel has almost turned full circle. We are now in the position of Charlotte's original readers, not knowing quite what to make of *Jane Eyre*, being generally disposed to admire, but a little baffled by the novel's strangeness. We do have some reservations, not of course those expressed by Lady Eastlake, but it is possible to dismiss some of these fairly rapidly. Most of us read and like *Jane Eyre* at a comparatively tender age, and we are reluctant to admit that our mature critical judgement cannot correct these early impressions; what we find exciting at the age of ten, namely the story with its episodic shifts of scene and preposterous coincidences, is obviously what is wrong with *Jane Eyre*, but then it is not just an adventure story for children, and in finding fault with the blemishes we have admired we ignore what we should be admiring.

We are also reluctant to find ourselves in agreement with the taste of the Victorians, although here it is important to be clear about the exact place of *Jane Eyre* in Victorian fiction, a place carefully mapped by K. Tillotson in *Novels of the 1840s*. As a pioneer in breaking away from the conventionalities of the Silver Fork School into a frank first-person narrative with the narrator giving full rein to her feelings, Charlotte was fortunate in the short run; her work was rightly hailed as original, although some found it too original. In the long run when she had attracted both good imitators who, as G. H. Lewes advised George Eliot,[2] made *Jane Eyre* their model but tried to improve upon it by righting the obvious faults in design, and inferior imitators who followed the outward trappings of *Jane Eyre* without the interior vision, the timing and even the success of the novel tells against its critical reputation. Weighed in the balance against the great realist novels of the nineteenth century like *War and Peace* and *Middlemarch*, *Jane Eyre* is obviously found wanting, but we wonder what Charlotte Brontë would have done had she had George Eliot's opportunities to study her predecessors. Weighed in the balance against the novels of Rhoda Broughton and indeed the whole world of escapist sub-literature, Charlotte is obviously superior; but equally obviously, we damage Charlotte by putting forward this category, and we wonder how Charlotte would have shown her originality had she written after and not before those who made characters like Mr. Rochester seem a preposterous convention.

If Mrs. Gaskell is to be believed, *Jane Eyre* was started in August 1846, nearly completed at the beginning of August 1847, and despatched to Smith, Elder on August 24th.[3] The story of its acceptance and rapid publication on October 10th, 1847, is a heartening gleam in the drab Brontë story, but those who have written and rewritten the tale, though they are entitled to make much of the publication of Charlotte's first novel, have done *Jane Eyre* a disservice by linking it so closely with Charlotte's biography. Thackeray's cavalier boast that he had met Jane Eyre, and Mrs. Gaskell's close identification of scenes in *Jane Eyre* with scenes in Charlotte's life, are typical of the biographical approach which wastes time in finding a real-life model for St. John Rivers, or measuring up the battlements of houses that might have been models for Thornfield. This approach has not encouraged serious critics of the novels.[4] While she was engaged on the novel, Charlotte's main concerns were her father's health, her brother's behaviour, the rejection of her first novel, and nagging doubts about the role of the single woman as the possibility of marriage receded and it seemed probable that all three sisters might soon be forced to earn their living. Only the most fanciful biographer dares to see much connection between Mr. Brontë's sight and Mr. Rochester's blindness, or Branwell's intoxication and the drunkenness of Mrs. Rochester, although we could say that the afflictions of her father and brother enabled Charlotte to give an accurate portrait of both drunkenness and recovery from blindness and may have prompted psychological and symbolic speculation. It is quite impossible to see any trace of Charlotte's feelings about the rejection of *The Professor* in *Jane Eyre*, and though there are reflections on the lot of women and the need for a single woman to earn her living by teaching, these are far less pointed than similar statements in *Shirley* and *Villette* written at a time when Charlotte had found both a vocation and a livelihood as an author. Thus *Jane Eyre*, in spite of its subtitle "An Autobiography," would seem to be Charlotte's least autobiographical novel, and it would be a great pity if the scenes at Lowood which must reflect, albeit hazily, Charlotte's memories of Cowan Bridge coloured our feeling for the whole novel.

Hostility to autobiography and the Brontë cult, as well as reaction against our childhood taste and against Victorian taste, may explain the severity of the criticisms which have been levelled against *Jane Eyre*. The story is an episodic one, though Charlotte's failing here is less grievous than in other novels because the personality of Jane acts as a unifying force. The plot of *Jane Eyre* is said to be incoherent and unlikely; wild coincidences abound, and Mr. Rochester is the most selfish and the most stupid of heroes in wanting to marry Jane with his mad wife in the house and thinking he can get away with it. This defect in so major a character draws our attention to the ambiguities in the position of both Miss Temple and Miss Fairfax, and even such important characters as Helen Burns and St. John Rivers are uncertainly placed. As a novel of protest against the way the upper classes treated their governesses or the way hypocritical schoolmasters maltreated their charges, *Jane Eyre* fails because its satire is so heavy-handed: we laugh at Mr. Brocklehurst and Baroness Ingram of Ingram Park, but we laugh for the wrong reasons. Unfortunately, it is not only in the scenes of satire that the language of *Jane Eyre* verges on the ridiculous: there is a strongly fustian element about some of Rochester's early declarations of love; Adèle's prattlings, most of which are in French, are unconvincing; and some of Charlotte's addresses to the reader are a little heavy-handed. Even the wholly admirable Gateshead section is disfigured by the following reflection, pompous in style and distorted in syntax.

"Unjust!—unjust!" said my reason, forced by the agonising stimulus into precocious though transitory power; and Resolve, equally wrought up, instigated some strange expedient to achieve escape from insupportable oppression—as running away, or, if that could not be effected, never eating or drinking more, and letting myself die. (JE., p. 11)

These charges are not easily met by a summary of the well-known story, which tends to throw them up more starkly. Jane Eyre, an orphan, is ill-treated by her aunt Mrs. Reed, and bullied by her cousins John, Eliza, and Georgiana. After rebelling against this treatment she is locked in the red room where her uncle had died, and thinks she sees his ghost. Her fright causes some alarm, and the apothecary, Mr. Lloyd, is sent for. He suggests that she should go to school, and the frightening Mr. Brocklehurst, headmaster of Lowood school, calls. Jane goes off to school on the first of many long journeys; at Lowood she is struck by the poor food and harsh conditions in which the pupils are forced to live. The superintendent, Miss Temple, is kind, but one of the teachers, Miss Scatcherd, is harsh to the girls, treating one virtuous pupil, Helen Burns, with special severity. Helen bears her unjust punishments with fortitude and is a comfort to Jane when Mr. Brocklehurst on a visit to the school accuses Jane of being a liar, although Miss Temple soon clears her of this charge. With the coming of spring, conditions slightly improve, but an epidemic strikes the school, claiming Helen Burns as one of its victims. The epidemic forces Mr. Brocklehurst to mend his ways, conditions at the school become better, and Jane spends eight reasonably contented years at Lowood, the last two as a teacher. On the departure of Miss Temple to be married, Jane becomes restless, advertises her services, and accepts a post at Thornfield, seventy miles away. No communications have all this time passed between Mrs. Reed and her niece, but just before she leaves Lowood, Jane meets Bessie, a servant from Gateshead, the only person who had been kind to her, and we learn from her that the fortunes of the Reeds are not prospering.

The Reeds are soon forgotten on Jane's arrival at Thornfield, which is a romantic old hall with rooks and battlements. The lady who had answered Jane's advertisement, Mrs. Fairfax, turns out to be not the owner of the house but only the housekeeper of a Mr. Rochester, whose ward Adèle is to be Jane's pupil. Jane gets on comfortably with Mrs. Fairfax and Adèle, but feels vaguely dissatisfied; she is curious about the mysterious third storey of Thornfield, from which there emerges a sinister laugh, and also about the personality of her master. Here her curiosity is soon satisfied. One evening while out alone she meets Mr. Rochester in a romantic setting, although rather unromantically, he then falls from his horse. Jane comes to his rescue, thus establishing herself on a friendly footing with her master and giving a hint of the useful if unromantic part she plays at the end of the novel. In the next few weeks he chats freely with Jane, explaining the origin of Adèle, the daughter of his mistress, and these intimate revelations, which shocked some Victorian readers, are followed by further intimacies when in the middle of the night Jane hears the sinister laugh again, discovers her master's bed on fire, and sensibly if un-

conventionally rushes in to quench the flames. There is obviously
a mystery about the third floor, although the only person who
seems to live there, a stolid-looking servant called Grace Poole,
hardly seems an adequate explanation for the mystery. Jane is
excited by her conversations with Mr. Rochester, but is somewhat
disappointed when he leaves the house the next day and returns
shortly with a fashionable house party, one of whom, Blanche
Ingram, is confidently expected to marry him. The house party
engage in trivial conversation, play charades, are rude about governesses, and treat Jane with disdain, but the arrival of a gypsy
fortune-teller who turns out to be Rochester in disguise alters the
situation, although Jane is very cautious in the replies she gives to
the probings of the supposed gypsy. Rochester is disturbed when
Jane tells him of the arrival of a guest called Mr. Mason, and that
very night there is a further commotion which Rochester conceals
from all except Jane; she helps him bind the wounds of Mr. Mason,
who has been cut and bitten in the shoulder; once again Grace
Poole is apparently to blame, although mysterious hints from the
two men make Jane dissatisfied with this explanation. Jane and
Rochester are drawn close together by this incident, but he seems
certain to marry Miss Ingram.

The tension slackens slightly when Bessie's husband, the coach-
man at Gateshead, arrives to summon Jane to her aunt's house.
John Reed has committed suicide, and Mrs. Reed is very ill. At
Gateshead Jane finds that Eliza has become a dry Anglo-Catholic
and Georgiana an overblown, fashionable beauty. The sisters
neglect their dying mother, and are heartily sick of each other;
Mrs. Reed, after confessing that she has neglected to inform Jane
of a letter from her father's brother, John Eyre, asking for her
whereabouts, dies, and, though she later writes to her uncle with
fateful results, Jane forgives her. After this episode Jane returns to
Thornfield to find that the house party has gone: Mr. Rochester
treats her very kindly, and Jane, now openly confessing her love for
her master, is happy, although still aware that the impending
marriage to Blanche Ingram must bring her happiness to an end.
On Midsummer Eve, Rochester, after teasing Jane about her impending departure, forces her to confess her love and asks her to
marry him. Jane accepts, although grim omens, like the splitting
of the great chestnut tree under which Rochester had proposed

and Mrs. Fairfax's anxious looks, seem to bode ill. Two nights before the wedding Jane is troubled by bad dreams, and sees an evil woman tear her wedding veil in two; she finds the wedding veil so torn in the morning. Rochester tries to comfort her, but we are not surprised that when Jane and Rochester go to the church to be married, the service is interrupted by two men. They reveal that the mysterious apparition in the top storey is Rochester's first wife, and this is confirmed when the abortive wedding party returns to Thornfield. Rochester reveals his wife in all her horror, Jane struggles heroically with her conscience and the pleas of Rochester that she should become his mistress, and the situation is resolved by her stealing out of the house in the early dawn.

After some days wandering, Jane is fortunate to be taken in by a clergyman and his two sisters, who turn out to be Jane's first cousins. Of all the coincidences in the novel this is the most shocking, although the shock is lessened by being delayed for some time, in which we get to know something of the Rivers family. The gentle sisters, Diana and Mary, are forced to leave their home to become governesses, while the sterner St. John is obviously anxious to become a missionary, although he could have saved the family fortunes by marrying Rosamund Oliver, the daughter of a rich manufacturer. Jane herself earns her living by teaching in the village school, but all these duties except St. John Rivers's vocation are solved by a remarkable discovery. Jane's uncle, John Eyre, who had through his knowledge of Mr. Mason, Mrs. Rochester's brother, prevented the bigamous marriage, has left Jane twenty thousand pounds; this discovery comes about because John Eyre is also the uncle of St. John and his sisters. Jane very properly shares out her money among her cousins, but St. John is not deterred from becoming a missionary; indeed he is perhaps prompted by the new-found family wealth to propose a loveless marriage to Jane. Jane is tempted, but is prevented from accepting by what some have thought another improbable feature, a mysterious call from Mr. Rochester. St. John bears his refusal well, but shows his resemblance to Mr. Brocklehurst by preaching a sermon in which he interprets Jane's refusal to accept the summons to follow him to India as a sign of her impending damnation.

Jane is undeterred, and as soon as possible, rejoicing in her new financial independence, returns to Thornfield, only to find it burnt to the ground. She learns from a garrulous innkeeper that this disaster is the final escapade of Mrs. Rochester, who had died in the fire, while Mr. Rochester had been blinded and maimed in his efforts to save her. Jane proceeds to the isolated house to which Rochester has retreated, there is a touching reunion, the pair are hastily married, and to complete a happy ending which even the most cynical critic cannot find inappropriate, Rochester partly recovers his sight.

All Charlotte's novels are episodic, and it is often difficult to see the connection between one episode and another, or the relevance of one particular episode. This charge cannot be levelled against *Jane Eyre*, where the personality of the heroine holds the novel together, and each separate episode is necessary to establish the singleness of this personality. We can ask ourselves how much *The Professor* would have gained by the omission of the early episodes in England, and we can equally ask how much *Jane Eyre* would have lost by the omission of the chapters concerning Gateshead and Lowood. In these chapters we learn to trust and to like Jane the narrator because she is so honest about her youthful short-comings, and to pity and sympathise with Jane the child, whose loneliness is so movingly described. A sensitive critic must agree with the most uncritical reader in being deeply impressed by the passage in which Jane describes the only happiness she found at Gateshead:

To this crib I always took my doll; human beings must love some-thing, and in the dearth of worthier objects of affection, I contrived to find a pleasure in loving and cherishing a faded graven image, shabby as a miniature scarecrow. It puzzles me now to remember with what absurd sincerity I doated on this little toy, half fancying it alive and capable of sensation. I could not sleep unless it was folded in my night-gown; and when it lay there safe and warm, I was comparatively happy, believing it to be happy likewise. (JE., p. 27)

Nor of course is Jane's unhappiness at Lowood simply a repetition of what she suffered at Gateshead. The two episodes are different because the wickedness of the Reeds is unthinking selfishness, while the wickedness of Mr. Brocklehurst is calculated hypocrisy. Jane reacts passionately against the former, but is tempted, follow-ing the example of Helen Burns, and to a lesser extent, Miss

Temple, to quell her natural rebelliousness against the Lowood system. Obviously the first and second sections of the book prefigure the third and fourth. Rochester's selfish passion and Jane's response to it are dangers which Jane must pass through as she passed through Gateshead, and St. John Rivers's inhumanity must be faced, not submitted to, in the same way as Lowood must be endured with courageous resistance, not suffered with crushed humility. But clearly the equation is not quite so crude as this; there is much of Helen Burns in St. John Rivers, both practicing a form of unworldliness which Jane admires, although she knows it is not for her, and Mr. Rochester is not of course a grasping bully. Moreover each section prepares Jane and the reader for the next. At Gateshead she learns self-mastery to prepare her for the ordeal of Lowood; at Lowood she learns Christian fortitude to prepare her for the temptations of love without marriage provided by Mr. Rochester; at Thornfield she learns what she wants in life to prepare her for the opposite temptation of marriage without love offered by St. John Rivers; and the whole range of her experience prepares her for the happy reconciliation between passion and duty at Ferndean.[5] At times the struggle between passion and duty almost seems like an allegorical psychomachia, although Charlotte's main aim is to show Jane's growing psychological maturity.

Other unifying elements are the images which recur at significant points in the narrative. The image of fire, standing for passion both as a destructive force and as a life-giving force against the cold which emanates from Lowood and to a lesser extent from Morton, is an obvious one, and this and other elemental symbols have been well explored.[6] The reference to pictures provides another recurring image, but because of the romantic, almost surrealistic obscurity of the pictures they are a little less easy to explain.[7] It would seem that Jane's exploration of Bewick's birds at Gateshead and the later sinister pictures she shows to Rochester are indications of the unchecked abandonment to feeling, the meaningless romanticism against which Jane must fight. Equally the sketching of cottages which is all the drawing permitted at Lowood and the portrait of Rosamund Oliver which Jane completes at Morton are insufficient exercises for her talent, and perhaps the following passage at the end of the novel shows the way in which Jane is able to fulfil her artistic talent and channel her romanticism into a useful outlet in real life:

He saw nature—he saw books through me; and never did I weary of gazing for his behalf, and of putting into words the effect of field, tree, town, river, cloud, sunbeam—of the landscape before us; of the weather round us—and impressing by sound on his ear what light could no longer stamp on his eye. (JE., p. 553)

These and other images obviously give both a pattern and a meaning to *Jane Eyre*, and the charge of fragmentation is an absurd one. Since the book is concerned with an interior struggle rather than a series of external events, the charge of improbability is less serious, though it must still be met. It is of course convenient that John Eyre, to whom Jane writes about her impending marriage, should, like a deus ex machina, both know Mr. Mason, and thus be able to rescue his niece from a bigamous marriage, and inform Jane that the Rivers were her cousins, leaving her twenty thousand pounds as well. Fortunate things do happen, and the granting of financial independence is an important ironic and economic point, because it enables us to contrast the inferior status of Jane at Thornfield with the full equality she attains at Ferndean. The cousinship between the Rivers family and Jane is less satisfactory because it is apparently unnecessary. We are, it is true, meant to contrast the charitable Rivers with the cruel Reeds, but this contrast would perhaps be more pointed if the Rivers were not cousins, and a comparison between the physical bullying of John Reed and the spiritual bullying of St. John Rivers is a little strained. Unlike the recognition scene in *Villette*, where Lucy Snowe in a similar state of collapse is fortunate enough to be rescued by the only people in the world with whom she has any ties, the reader is ill prepared to discover that Jane has found her first cousins because we never knew she had any cousins apart from the Reeds, and on a realistic level we are bound to ask why the Rivers family with their charitable instincts did not take more interest in their cousin at an earlier stage. John Eyre in Madeira seems more anxious about Jane Eyre than is St. John Rivers with his eyes set on India, and perhaps we are meant to learn something from this contrast, although Charlotte is more at pains to stress rather snobbishly the good lineage of the Rivers family, thus establishing Jane's claims to gentility, as well as the superiority of the Rivers over the Reeds.

The parallel between St. John Rivers and John Bretton in *Villette* must not be stressed too closely, because though both are handsome, both rescue the heroine when she is in distress, and both turn out to be the wrong man for her, Lucy Snowe is clearly in love with John Bretton in spite of his slight narrowness of vision, while Jane Eyre is prevented by St. John Rivers's crippling religious strictness from ever loving him, and in any case she, unlike Lucy, has already fallen in love with somebody else. Nevertheless, the recognition scene in *Villette* does suggest that making St. John Rivers and Jane Eyre cousins may have a purpose. Both Lucy Snowe and Jane Eyre are very lonely: this is obviously true of Lucy, and even at Thornfield the slightly less solitary Jane is not fully at ease with Mrs. Fairfax and Adèle, she is despised by the house party, and the affection she receives from Rochester is dishonourable. Thus the entry of both heroines into families with whom they have a well-established bond is a landmark in their progress away from loneliness, and the temptation both heroines face is to see this landmark as their final goal. Mrs. Bretton and the Rivers sisters, with whom Jane's relationship is always good, stand for friendship; St. John Rivers and John Bretton show the dangers of confusing friendship with love. Improbable though it is that Jane Eyre should choose her cousins' house as a place for her collapse, the fact that the Rivers *are* her cousins enables Jane and the reader both to measure her spiritual progress and to judge how far she has to go.

The main section of the novel occurs at Thornfield, and here the improbabilities centre on Mr. Rochester's mad wife. The existence of such a creature is certainly possible; and, after the discovery of various Victorian skeletons, we are perhaps better able than Mrs. Humphry Ward to appreciate that it is quite likely that Mr. Rochester could have hoped to get away with concealing the presence of his wife. Only Mr. Mason could have revealed that she was his wife, for people like Mrs. Fairfax would know that there was some mystery, but Victorian reticence would have prevented her from probing further, and certainly from burdening the delicate ears of Jane Eyre with any dark tales. Of course Jane cannot help using her imagination and weaving fantasies around the unromantic Grace Poole. Unlike Catherine Morland in *Northanger Abbey*, who is right in thinking that there is something sinister about General Tilney but wrong in thinking that he has murdered his wife, Jane has Gothic fantasies about Grace Poole that turn out to be less terrible than the real Bertha Rochester; although, as admirers of Charlotte's use of the Gothic style have pointed out, Charlotte is quick to show the squalid realities behind the Gothic apparition.[8]

We are also in a somewhat different position from Victorian critics when it comes to a discussion of the probability of Mr. Rochester's wish to deceive Jane Eyre into a false marriage. Charlotte has to strike a delicate balance between making Rochester so wicked that we cannot understand Jane's admiration for him and making him not wicked enough for us to be able to understand Jane's reluctance to become his mistress. Some nineteenth-century critics (and Mrs. Humphry Ward) thought Rochester's crime put him beyond the pale, and some modern readers (and George Eliot) cannot see what all the fuss was about,[9] but most Victorian readers and most modern readers aware of Victorian conventions think that Charlotte strikes the balance fairly well. Jane could have accepted Rochester's offer to defy convention—which, in the shape of the cruelty at Gateshead, the hypocrisy of Lowood, and the frivolity of the house party, has not appeared in a very good light—whereas the unconventional behaviour of Rochester in discussing his mistresses is part of his charm. On the other hand these discussions show Jane the dangers of becoming another Céline Varens, and Adèle's listless prattle remind us of the dangers of having and being an illegitimate child; it is significantly of a little child that Jane dreams so often, and to a suffering child that Jane compares her lost love when she knows that Rochester has betrayed her. For betrayed her he has, not just in offering her a bigamous marriage, or in withholding the truth about his first wife at an earlier stage, but in trying, by such devices as buying Jane smart clothes which she does not want, to shore up a relationship that is founded on falsehood.

And it is in the context of falsehood that we want to look at the house-party scenes which attracted adverse comments from some reviewers who perhaps thought they were being satirised, and which have attracted equally adverse comments from those who do not mind Charlotte satirising the Victorian upper classes, but do mind that she does it so badly. Charlotte knew very little of the behaviour of the upper classes, her own experiences having been on a more humble level, and she had read few of the Silver Fork novels in which the behaviour of the aristocracy was chronicled in rather a stilted fashion. Inevitably, therefore, the house party with its absurd charades and bogus fortune-teller jars a little, but this does not really matter, as Charlotte is intent on describing the web of falsity in which her two main characters are caught. Nor is the irony altogether unsubtle. The charade is built round the word Bridewell, and Jane, thinking Rochester is intent on marrying Blanche Ingram, says, "Your bride stands between us." These seem to be rather obvious references to Rochester's bigamy, and equally obvious are the physical resemblances between Bertha Rochester and Blanche Ingram: Charlotte did not like big strapping women. Charlotte is not, however, simply trying to be crudely clever in making these obvious points. She is both creating sympathy for Rochester, as she shows him desperately juggling with Bertha his real wife, Blanche the person whom he is expected to marry, and Jane whom he wants to marry, and showing that this sympathy cannot allow us to forget that Rochester intends to commit bigamy. Blanche Ingram is a very useful character, not only because like Mrs. Rochester she has material attractions and coarsely sensual charms, in resisting which Mr. Rochester obviously does well, but also because it sometimes seems that Rochester is simply trying to replace Blanche Ingram with Jane Eyre, thus doing irretrievable harm to the real bond between him and Jane, a bond which transcends material or sensual satisfaction.

Charlotte's style in *Jane Eyre* is not without its blemishes, but, as has been pointed out, the perversion of word order and frequent negatives are a useful method of demonstrating Jane's originality and rejection of convention.[10] Nor are the pompous circumlocutions without their purpose, since Charlotte frequently uses them not to express her own views, but to demonstrate the falsity of her characters' ideals, as she shows when she brings them down to earth. When Bessie and Abbot are discussing Jane's sad story, Abbot is made to say, "If she were a nice pretty child, one might compassionate her forlornness," but the unreality of this sentiment is shown when she finishes her sentence, "but one really cannot care for such a little toad as that." Abbot goes on to utter a statement that is reminiscent of Rodolphe's declaration of love for Emma Bovary amidst the cries of the market place:

"Yes, I dote on Miss Georgiana. . . . Little darling!—with her long curls and her blue eyes, and such a sweet colour as she has; just as if she were painted!—Bessie, I could fancy a Welsh rabbit for supper." (JE., p. 24)

Charlotte's confidential remarks to her audience, culminating in the famous "Reader, I married him," have been a source of embarrassment to some readers who have seen these nudges as a rather unfair attempt to establish a cosy relationship between reader and narrator. In view of Charlotte's difficulty about establishing a proper narrative method, as shown by the eccentricities of the juvenilia, and the clumsiness of *The Professor* and *Shirley*, it seems surprising that *Jane Eyre* should be so successful. Certainly when we are addressed as readers in *Jane Eyre* we rarely feel the intrusiveness we feel when Richardson's Pamela explains how she is managing her correspondence, or when Thackeray steps aside from his narrative to say that he is inventing the whole thing. The remarks to the reader seem to follow no particular pattern, occurring both at moments of high tension—as when Jane leaves Thornfield for Morton—and of low tension—as when she leaves Lowood for Thornfield—but they do all serve to establish Jane's honesty both as a protagonist and as a narrator.

The distinction between the Jane who as child and governess suffers the adventures described in *Jane Eyre*, and the happily married woman of about thirty who narrates these adventures is an important one, because the book aims to show the one growing through harsh experience into maturity as the other. The honesty of Jane as a child in admitting her faults, at Thornfield in confessing so early her love for Mr. Rochester, and at Morton in admitting that she felt degraded by her work as a schoolmistress is obvious, and it is one reason why we are so ready to accept the improbabilities the story contains, even the fantastic telepathy which Rochester uses to prevent Jane from marrying St. John Rivers. The honesty of the narrator is more in question. Essentially, like all narrators, the thirty-year-old Jane Eyre is being secretive in not telling us what she knows: namely, that Rochester's first attempt to marry Jane will not work but that it will all come out right in the end. The bad omens at Thornfield and frequent mentions of Mr. Rochester's name at Morton give us some fairly good hints on both these scores, although to give more away would obviously be to destroy the excitement of the story. Indeed, the narrative is full of skilful suspense, as when Jane returns to find Thornfield burnt down and the innkeeper insists on telling her what she knows already before getting down to the history of the fire.

In *Villette* Lucy Snowe is a secretive protagonist, and, although used to the plain dealing of *Jane Eyre,* we find the contortions in the narrative disturbing, they are somehow suitable as emerging from the mature Lucy Snowe. In *Jane Eyre* the narrator does her best to keep faith with us, and the addresses to the reader are part of this process. The first Mrs. Rochester manages to break into Jane's room and tear her wedding veil two nights before the wedding; this is a powerful scene with strong symbolic overtones, and one may ask why Charlotte did not set it in the night before the wedding. The answer to this is that Mr. Rochester would hardly be away from home on that night, and that if he had been at home Jane would at once have demanded an explanation from him, which might have precipitated the discovery of Mrs. Rochester's identity. As it is, the force of the description is not lost because Jane does not describe what has happened until the next evening when Rochester returns home. Jane, the narrator, feels bound to apologise for the delay: "Stay till he comes, reader; and when I disclose my secret to him, you shall share the confidence" (JE., p. 335). The reader is thus enabled not only to share Jane's undefined feeling of dread as she waits anxiously for Rochester to return, but to hear the story of the apparition the night before the wedding and to feel a distinct feeling of unease at Rochester's rather frantic explanation.

It is impossible not to like Jane Eyre, to share her disappointments, to sympathise with her aspirations, and to rejoice that eventually her hopes are rewarded. Such is the strength of her character and such the force of the narrative that even on reading the book for the third or fourth time we still hope against hope that the first wedding will come off, and still have our fears that Jane may chain herself to the glacial St. John Rivers. Jane's frankness about her love for Rochester although he is not handsome, and her inability to love St. John Rivers although he is handsome, her fears that Rochester may try to make her his mistress before they are married, and her anxiety that he may try to rape her after the marriage has failed, is by Victorian standards highly refreshing. So too is her insistence on full equality in marriage: it is one of St. John Rivers's troubles that he tries to crush Jane into nothingness by means of his iron will, while Rochester even at Thornfield allows Jane to have her own way on most points, because in spite of the pert exchanges there is no real difference between them.

Readers have been less kind to Edward Fairfax Rochester, seen by some as a preposterous unreal figure[11] stepping straight out of the pages of one of Charlotte's Angrian chronicles. It is of course Blanche Ingram who compares Rochester to Byron's Corsair, and it is Charlotte's purpose to pierce through the Angrian or Byronic glamour to the reality beneath. Initially Jane sees Rochester in a romantic setting accompanied by a Gytrash: the Gytrash turns out to be a friendly dog, and Jane's first service to this romantic figure is the prosaic one of rendering him assistance when he has fallen from his horse. Rochester's statements about Jane bewitching him like a fairy, and his revelations about his past, do ring a little false, but perhaps they are meant to appear false, showing that Rochester is still putting on a mask to disguise the hideous reality which is well shown in the lurid tawdriness of the description of Rochester's time in the West Indies. Shortly after this Jane says, "Reader, I forgave him," and most of us would be prepared to do the same. Some have accused him of male chauvinism, of exploiting Jane's weakness when he calls her poor and obscure and small and plain, but when he does so he is using Jane's own words. Some have seen the blinding and maiming of Rochester as a crude device, both paying lip-service to the Victorian convention that sexual misdemeanours must be punished, and bringing Rochester down to Jane's level, so that this time he is poor and obscure and blind and plain, but the punishment of Rochester does have the effect of showing once and for all that the bond between him and Jane is a true one, above such considerations as physical beauty or material wealth.[12]

Rochester convinces us because we see him through Jane's eyes; a third-person narrator would make him as ridiculous as Zamorna or the Corsair on which Blanche Ingram dotes. Jane is perhaps less successful in persuading us of the merits of St. John Rivers as a realistic character. One feels at times that the remarks about St. John being a great and good man are made neither by the nineteen-year-old Jane nor by the thirty-year-old Jane, but by Charlotte anxious to placate contemporary taste—although two contemporary readers, Thackeray and Mary Taylor, roundly condemned the portrait of St. John Rivers as a failure. In *Villette* Lucy Snowe occasionally interrupts her narrative to say that John Bretton was not as good as she had painted him, and the praise of St. John Rivers seems a similar kind of intrusion. In a way Charlotte is trying to combine in St. John the self-satisfaction of Mr. Brocklehurst and the self-sacrifice of Helen Burns and Miss Temple, and though the pillar imagery and the frequent references to cold obviously associate St. John with the former[13] there are plenty of features about him which we can admire. He is without hypocrisy, in that unlike Mr. Brocklehurst he practices what he preaches; he is never openly cruel or brutal; his self-restraint is admirable; and both in the discovery of Jane's identity and in his rejection of Jane's idea that they should go to India without marrying, he displays a brisk common sense which Mr. Brocklehurst with his impractical ideas on how to run a school wholly lacks. His good looks are also stressed, and this does not remind us either of the grim Mr. Brocklehurst or the bloated John Reed. In addition, St. John's association with the gentle Mary and spirited Diana Rivers is obviously a factor in his favour. Nevertheless, we would be fairly confident that St. John was not meant to be on the side of the angels if Charlotte had not ended the novel with an account of his heroic travail and impending early death.

Charlotte never seemed sure whether it was in this world or the next that happiness was to be won. In her later novels and in a significant letter[14] she seemed very sceptical about the joys of this world, but in *Jane Eyre* until the last three paragraphs we could be fairly confident that Charlotte rejects the idea of striving for a heavenly crown as a refined form of selfishness. Perhaps we can follow the pervasive Eden imagery to work out what Charlotte is trying to say through St. John Rivers; it is a little fanciful to use his surname as a pointer to the rivers with which the Garden of Eden is surrounded, although there may be some meaning behind his name and that of the Reeds. Jane and Rochester are in a transitory paradise at Thornfield, and with lingering steps and slow Jane has to leave. But this is a fortunate fall because she eventually re-enters, after passing through the final trial of St. John Rivers's courtship, a more lasting and durable paradise at Ferndean. And yet Charlotte evidently did not feel that the life of the Rochesters amid the trees and fields of Ferndean was a totally satisfactory symbol of the joys of heaven, and she felt bound to add the description of St. John's missionary endeavours as a pointer both to what the Rochesters had achieved and to what they were aiming. St. John Rivers is both an obstacle to Jane's self-fulfilment and at the same time a symbol of this fulfilment, and it is because he has to play this dual role in the book that he is something of a failure.

Jane's other cousins, the Reeds, also play a dual role, but they are more successfully conceived. Charlotte had not much experience of the world, but she knew something of the heartless selfishness of children, and few would dispute that on a realistic level the Gateshead scenes at the beginning of the book succeed admirably. Jane is also made to return to Gateshead in the middle of the Thornfield section. This may seem a crude device for cranking up the plot, so that Jane can get in touch with her uncle John Eyre, who can prevent her marriage; it also enables the tension building up at Thornfield to be suspended, and incidentally shows how far Jane has progressed from being the humiliated and unhappy child that she was in the first chapter. But the character sketches of Georgiana and Eliza Reed serve another function: they represent the extremes of total self-indulgence and useless self-sacrifice to which Jane is at various times tempted. Georgiana's vacuous gossip is presented in fairly conventional terms, but with Eliza, Charlotte is obviously doing more than work off her prejudice against Roman and Anglo-Catholicism. Eliza is cruel and heartless both to her mother and to her sister; she is busy all day and yet achieves little. Early in the book she is shown as having a mercenary nature, and it is obvious that she has merely changed from calculating how much money she will get from her poultry to calculating what reward in heaven she will receive from her devotions. It is tempting at times to see something of Eliza Reed both in St. John Rivers and in the dried-up missionary that Jane Eyre would be if she went to India, although Charlotte's religious beliefs would not allow her to believe that the valuable task of spreading the gospel among the heathen could be compared to life as a nun.

A comparison between Helen Burns and St. John Rivers is much easier to make. Both seek the heavenly crown, and neither seems afraid of an early death. The equation of Helen Burns with Maria Brontë has obscured the resemblance, and it is also much more obvious that Helen, Jane's first friend who listens to her fretfulness with quiet patience, is an agent in her progress rather than an obstacle. If Jane had not met Helen, she would have remained the lonely and bad-tempered child into which the ill-treatment she had received at Gateshead was rapidly turning her. Helen teaches Jane forgiveness for all, and she remembers this on Mrs. Reed's deathbed; Helen comforts Jane with the thought of eventual reunion in heaven, and she offers this crumb of comfort to Mr. Rochester at the crisis in their lives. Thus, although both their surnames are associated with water, since "burn" is a Scottish synonym for "brook," and as if to drive home the point about her name Helen daydreams of brooks, it may seem odd to compare Helen's saintliness with St. John's harshness. Yet Helen is not without a touch of sternness: just as St. John asks for a book after Jane has laboured so hard to refurbish Moor House, Helen prefers reading *Rasselas* to answering too many of Jane's questions; just as St. John urges Jane to wrench her heart from man, Helen tells Jane she thinks too much of the love of human beings. Both St. John and Helen harp rather boringly on their own shortcomings, which seem few and far between. Where the two differ is in their attitude towards evil. Whereas St. John, like Mr. Brocklehurst, appears to adopt the Calvinistic attitude of dividing people into sheep who are saved and goats who are damned, Helen preaches a Universalist attitude, whereby everybody is saved. Charlotte was obviously drawn to Helen's position, as a solution to the problems of life after death, but Helen's doctrine that we should forgive evil people on earth is less appealing. We cannot help feeling that Jane has a point when she says that turning the other cheek to evil doers only encourages them to sin all the more, and certainly Miss Scatcherd's bad temper seems to thrive on Helen's mildness.

To tolerate intolerance is a form of intolerance, and both Helen Burns and Miss Temple would seem to be guilty of just this. Helen, though she could object against Miss Scatcherd, could hardly do much in protesting against Mr. Brocklehurst; but Miss Temple could resign. Presumably, like many subordinates of evil men, she thought she could do more good by staying and alleviating the distress of the pupils than by a rash resignation which would leave her without a post. Charlotte Brontë does not raise these questions, although she does begin to explore the similarly equivocal position of Mrs. Fairfax, who can plead ignorance of Rochester's misdemeanours. Miss Temple is of course a limiting factor in Jane's life; she prepares her for little except becoming a schoolmistress like herself, and she does not prepare her well for that, since Jane is so dissatisfied when Miss Temple leaves to get married. Thus in spite of the praise lavished on her, we feel that Miss Temple is not as good as she is made out to be; in this she resembles St. John, as she resembles him in the following passage describing the repression of her feelings, when Mr. Brocklehurst is maintaining that bad food is good for the girls:

Miss Temple had looked down when he first began to speak to her; but she now gazed straight before her, and her face, naturally pale as marble, appeared to be assuming also the coldness and fixity of that material; especially her mouth, closed as if it would have required a sculptor's chisel to open it, and her brow settled gradually into petrified severity. (JE., pp. 70–71)

Miss Temple's inability to do anything about the food, except to provide some temporary palliatives, is explained by the fact that she has no control over the housekeeper, the appropriately named Mrs. Harden. But she should presumably have been able to exercise some control over the teaching staff, and in allowing Miss Scatcherd to punish Helen Burns, she was tolerating intolerance. Charlotte knew something about how schools were run; Mademoiselle Reuter and Madame Beck do not have many virtues, but they can conduct an efficient school, and Miss Temple seems to lack this virtue.

Thus it is not wholly unfair to compare Helen Burns and Miss Temple with St. John Rivers as potentially blighting influences on Jane Eyre's life. It is slightly unfair, though: whereas St. John comes out badly in contrast to the comforting presence of his sisters, Helen and Miss Temple are sources of kindness in contrast to the grim figure of Mr. Brocklehurst, the cause of the blight which hangs over Lowood. The line of hypocritical Evangelical clergyman in Victorian fiction is a long one, and the portrait of Mr. Brocklehurst lacks the depth of some of the later creations of Dickens, Thackeray, and Trollope.[15] Some of the satire directed against Mr. Brocklehurst seems so crude that we are tempted to think of him as a caricature, hardly suitable as a source of stultifying cruelty, and we would welcome more enquiry into the nature of his self-deception. On the other hand, in defence of Charlotte we must remember that the difference between Mr. Brocklehurst's treatment of his own family, who are allowed smart clothes and long ringlets, and the girls at Lowood, whose hair has to be cut short even when it curls naturally, is a pointer to the different treatment of the rich and the poor which was one of the less attractive features of Evangelicalism. One can hardly claim that Charlotte Brontë is a pioneer in social reform: indeed she makes Jane comment on several occasions that she did not want to be poor,[16] but at least she has the grace to protest against those who proclaim that some were chosen to be rich, some were not. In addition, an intense exploration of Mr. Brocklehurst's motives would be unsuitable if it came from a child of ten, and it is because we see Mr. Brocklehurst only through Jane's eyes without comment from author or narrator that he remains what he is meant to be, a figure of terror, a figure of evil.

It is of course true that to understand Mr. Brocklehurst we have to know something of Victorian religion. He is a pointer to the fact that *Jane Eyre* inevitably lacks the universality of *Wuthering Heights*. In spite of a certain ambiguity about the position of the poor and conventional religion, *Jane Eyre* is characterised by a sense of absolute justice; this strongly marked feeling for right and wrong is again a contrast with *Wuthering Heights*, where Emily's central moral position is impossible to fathom, though she can make clear statements on minor issues. The intensity of Charlotte's feelings is matched by the clarity with which she expresses them, and this has proved a disadvantage with some readers for whom *Jane Eyre* has proved too obvious and too narrow. *Jane Eyre* does not grapple with the cosmic problems of *Wuthering Heights*, it does not cover the wide range of human society depicted in *Middlemarch*, it does not even explore obscure recesses of the human personality like *Villette*. And yet once we have thrown off the notion that the novel is a child's adventure story or a series of autobiographical episodes, *Jane Eyre* can and should be seen as a deeply satisfying statement of one person's solution to the problem of keeping a proper balance between altruism and selfishness.

NINE

Shirley

Charlotte's publishers were eager for another novel after the success of *Jane Eyre*, but initially she made slow progress.[1] By the time of Branwell's death in September 1848 she had, according to Mrs. Gaskell, almost finished the second volume of *Shirley*; but she did not resume writing until the spring of 1849, although the novel was ready for the publishers at the end of August and was published on October 26th. Contemporary critics, who knew nothing of the harrowing circumstances in which *Shirley* was written, treated the work relatively kindly; there were the usual charges of coarseness and more pertinent accusations from G. H. Lewis to the effect that the novel lacked unity, but Victorian critics, perhaps because *Shirley* fulfilled more easily than either *Jane Eyre* or *Villette* the public expectation of what a novel should be, were reasonably impressed.[2] Modern critics have, however, been embarrassed by Charlotte's second published novel and have tended to ignore it; comments on *Shirley* have with a few exceptions been confined to discussions of its biographical relevance or historical accuracy, and these discussions have hardly helped to promote critical analysis.[3]

The biographers have indeed had a field day with *Shirley*, paying little heed to Charlotte's statement that "we only suffer reality to suggest, never to dictate." The resemblances between the landscape and houses in *Shirley* with the places in East Yorkshire where Ellen Nussey and Mary Taylor lived have been carefully charted, and the identification between the Taylor family and the Yorkes in *Shirley* has been taken for granted, although the Taylors themselves complained that the portrait was an inaccurate one.[4] Real-life models for Mr. Helstone and Robert Moore have been sought, although the insights which Charlotte displays into the character of these two men can hardly have come from historical knowledge or personal acquaintance. Caroline Helstone has been variously identified as Charlotte herself, Ellen Nussey, and Anne Brontë; the colour of Caroline's eyes changes in the course of the novel, and this has been taken as a sign that Charlotte, moved by Anne's sufferings, allowed autobiographical comment to dictate the form of the novel.[5] The statement by Mrs. Gaskell that the character of Shirley is Charlotte's representation of Emily, or more accurately of what Emily would have been had she been placed in health and prosperity, has been seized upon gratefully by biographical critics, although, as Mrs. Gaskell saw but these critics apparently do not, not only was Emily not rich or healthy; she was not beautiful or outspoken or cheerful either.

Historical comment on *Shirley* has confirmed the accuracy of Charlotte's description of the Luddite riots, and her just picture of the harshness and selfishness of the mill-owners on the one hand, and on the other the brutality and lawlessness of the workers.[6] She does accept too readily the conventional view that the workers were led astray by agitators, and that the Luddite movement was not a spontaneous one. There is little attempt to penetrate the motives of the workers and in particular their dislike of being reduced from skilled craftsmen to mere factory hands. An added complication in discussing Charlotte's accuracy is that when writing about the events of 1812 she has in mind the events of 1848 when revolutions broke out all over Europe, and Chartism threatened England. There is a not very well authenticated story that Charlotte originally intended to write about Chartism;[7] in any case, there are pointers to her concern with the present as well as the past in her frequent uncomplimentary references to the continent, and in her harping upon her childhood hero the Duke of Wellington, who was of course as active, though in a rather less glorious role, in 1848 as he was in 1812. Indeed a brave attempt has been made by the editors of the Penguin edition of *Shirley* to show that Charlotte's allusion to the death of Jessie Yorke in a foreign land, taken generally as a piece of purely autobiographical sentiment in memory of Martha Taylor, is a useful reminder that

126 THE BRONTËS

Charlotte may be writing about the past, but the sad present is with us now.[8] Charlotte's modesty about her own ability to .deal with matters of public interest may explain why she used the Luddite revolt as a mask under which she could show her concern about Chartism without inviting criticism from those who might attack her ignorance on current affairs.

By 1849 the threat of revolution in England had abated slightly, and this fact as well as her own private griefs may explain why Charlotte's concern with public affairs lapses in the second half of the novel. The problem of reconciling the story of the Luddites with the love affairs of Caroline Helstone and Shirley Keeldar has been the main focus for critical discussion, the lack of a first-person narrator being a subsidiary and complementary objection to *Shirley*. Biographical and historical discussions have tended to inflame our prejudices against *Shirley* as a novel, in which Charlotte put all the people she knew, set them in a historical context which she had read about in the newspapers, and then proceeded to work out her ideas on a number of contemporary topics. There is some force in these speculations, and there is no doubt that Charlotte was hamstrung by her decision to adopt a third-person narrator, but the usual charge that the novel lacks unity can be met.

Shirley opens promisingly with a description of a meeting of three silly young curates, Mr. Malone, Mr. Donne, and Mr. Sweeting. It could be argued that Charlotte never enlarges on the theme of the uselessness of the clergy, fiddling over trivial matters while England was threatened with burning revolution, and that she was not able to develop this theme, because though she is really concerned, as her first page makes out, with the triviality of the disciples of Newman and Pusey, her novel is concerned with 1812 when these disciples were in their cradles. Thus the curates, who appear almost as comic relief at odd intervals during the novel, never really play a major part, although it would not be wholly correct to say that Charlotte is not concerned throughout the novel with the limitations of the clergy. The curates are but pale imitations of their rectors, whom one day they will succeed, and indeed we are soon introduced to one of these rectors, Mr. Helstone, a man who in spite of many admirable qualities is as ineffective in solving the problems of the poor as he is inadequate in seeing what is wrong with his niece Caroline.

Mr. Helstone has come to fetch Malone in order that he may help defend Hollow's-mill against possible danger from Luddites. Malone goes to Hollow's-mill where he meets the owner, Robert Moore, but he is too late to prevent damage to Moore's machinery, which has been set upon by rioters. This discovery is reported by Mr. Yorke, a neighbouring mill-owner who shares Moore's desire for peace with the French but thinks he should act in a concilia-tory fashion to the workers. Mr. Helstone is a Tory, rejecting any idea of peace with Napoleon, and equally opposed to any weak-ness in face of Luddite threats. Thus, though the introduction of new characters is a little bewildering, and the political discussions may seem a little boring, Charlotte has contrived with remarkable economy to introduce three different political standpoints and to hint at a fourth view of her own that the war against Napoleon should be prosecuted with the utmost vigour, but that at home the workers should not be treated too harshly.

Miss Helstone's niece is then brought onto the stage, and per-haps rather rapidly we learn that she is in love with Robert Moore, who is her cousin. Robert seems at first to return her love but then cools, and political differences between him and Mr. Helstone prevent the pair from meeting. Caroline goes into a protracted decline, pining for Robert and bewailing her unhappy lot. Possible sources of relief are an interest in doing good works like Miss Ainley and Miss Mann, two virtuous old spinsters, and the com-pany of a neighbouring heiress, Miss Shirley Keeldar of Fieldhead, but these turn out to be counter-productive. Caroline, though she admires the old spinsters, does not wish to imitate their narrow outlook, and there seems a distinct possibility that Robert Moore will marry Shirley Keeldar, who is his landlord. During this section of the book Charlotte is handicapped by her narrative method. We are allowed access to the workings of Caroline's mind; she seems at times to be a meeker Jane Eyre, tempted to sacrifice her feelings but aware that this is an unsatisfactory course. We are not, however, although we have a supposedly omniscient narrator, allowed similar access to the mind of Robert Moore or Shirley Keeldar; it is not until later that we learn that it is financial stress which drives Robert to reject Caroline in favour of Shirley. As a result Robert's behaviour seems inexplicable and Shirley's conduct insensitive. In the former case our reaction to Robert coincides with that of Caroline, and there is no real awkwardness in the narrative, but the failure in communication between Shirley and Caroline does seem to point to the writer's inability to communicate with her readers.

Shirley has great gifts as an organiser and with some rather timid help from Caroline plays a prominent part in setting up a fund for the relief of the poor, and in arranging a Sunday School outing, in the course of which the Church of England party meets and routs a rival Nonconformist band. She also displays considerable courage in trying to warn Robert Moore of an attack on his mill, but, since Robert is aided by the local gentry and clergy, the attack is repulsed and Shirley's warning is not needed. The common enemy unites Moore and Helstone, and Caroline is able in the succeeding weeks to see a little more of her cousin, especially as Shirley is occupied with the arrival of her relatives, the Sympsons, at Fieldhead. It turns out that the tutor of the Sympson's son is none other than Robert's brother Louis. This coincidence is closely followed by another when Caroline falls ill, and it is revealed that Shirley's housekeeper Mrs. Pryor, who comes to nurse her, is none other than Caroline's own mother, formerly a governess who had married Mr. Helstone's dissipated younger brother. There are fewer coincidences in *Shirley* than in Charlotte's other works, and our dissatisfaction with the arrival of Mrs. Pryor and Louis Moore is probably caused by the unsatisfactory nature of both characters, who seem principally used as vehicles to express Charlotte's thoughts on the theme of the downtrodden governess.

Caroline's illness is a severe one, and her life hangs in the balance; but with Mrs. Pryor's help she recovers. Robert Moore has left home to hunt down the ringleaders of the attack on the mills and Shirley continues to be occupied with the Sympsons and a series of suitors. One of these, Sir Philip Nunnely, is thought on all sides to be a suitable match, but Shirley rejects him. Mr. Sympson believes that this is because she is in love with Robert Moore, but the reader has already heard Robert Moore confessing to Mr. Yorke that Shirley had turned him down, thinking with some justification that he was after her money. Shortly after this confession Robert Moore is shot and becomes gravely ill; thanks to Martin Yorke, Caroline is taken to his bedside, and as Charlotte puts it in one of her coy chapter headings, an unattractive feature of the book, "matters make some progress." It is revealed that Shirley's lover is Louis Moore; we learn this rather oddly from the pen of Louis himself, whose diary the reader has been previously privileged to read. Mr. Sympson objects furiously, but his objections are overruled, and since both Robert Moore's fortune and his standing with Mr. Helstone conveniently improve with the repeal of the Orders in Council, the way is open for a happy if unromantic double wedding.

The theme of the downtrodden governess is perhaps the easiest to extract from the rest of the book. We feel that Mrs. Pryor and, to a lesser extent, Louis Moore are unnecessary intrusions, and at times it seems as if Charlotte, whose publishers had not allowed her to print an answer to the harsh review of *Jane Eyre* in *The Quarterly Review*, had seized upon *Shirley* as a vehicle for paying back Lady Eastlake. If the imagined dialogue between Mrs. Pryor and her employers, the Hardmans, is a substitute for *A Word to The Quarterly*, then one can understand the reluctance of Smith and Elder to publish this reply, as the satire is heavy-handed.[9] Not all employers of governesses were so unfeeling as the Hardmans or Mr. Sympson, and Mrs. Pryor's crushed acceptance of the right of the Hardmans to trample upon her is in a sense counterproductive; we feel rather like Blanche Ingram that Mrs. Pryor is indeed a poor creature and deserves to be crushed, although her maiden name, Grey, reminds us of Anne's more spirited heroine. Yet Mrs. Pryor's subservience to the Hardmans does show that the governess theme is not as isolated from the rest of the novel as might appear. Caroline Helstone is in danger, as Jane Eyre was previously, of being crushed by the unfeeling behaviour of her uncle and cousin into accepting a destiny to which she is unsuited. She does ask her uncle whether she should take a post as a governess; he dismisses her question as feminine fancy, but we realise that if she had not married, Caroline would have had to seek employment as a governess.

Seen as part of a protest against the cripplingly narrow destiny allotted to women, the chapter about Mrs. Pryor's experiences fits in well with the rest of the novel, and it is Louis Moore, the tutor, who triumphantly turns the tables on his employer, that causes more difficulty. Like William Crimsworth, Louis Moore has many feminine qualities, and like Crimsworth, Moore shows that success in the teaching profession is possible; we feel that the success of both characters has a certain unreal quality about it because it is based on what Charlotte wished for herself, rather than what she had experienced. Unfortunately, as men Crimsworth and Moore are very unsatisfactory symbols for feminist aspirations. It almost looks as if Charlotte lacked the confidence to portray completely successful women. Those who have seized upon *Shirley* as a feminist novel, pointing out quite correctly the bitterness with which Charlotte Brontë indicates the limitations of Caroline Helstone's life, should note Charlotte's timidity in making Shirley, who can apparently surmount these limitations, eventually submit to the yoke of Louis Moore's will: "Never was wooer of wealthy bride so thoroughly absolved from the subaltern part; so inevitably compelled to assume a paramount character" (S., p. 657).

In spite of this seeming relapse into conventionality, Shirley obviously does give a fairly consistent feminist view.[10] Happy marriages in the book are the exception rather than the rule. Mr. Helstone despised his wife, Mrs. Pryor's husband was a scoundrel, and the Yorke family, thought by many to be a biographical excrescence, stresses the same point, both because Mrs. Yorke is so morose and because Rose Yorke displays the same original streak of independence as Mary Taylor. Caroline Helstone's unhappiness because she is not allowed to tell people of her love, and the contempt with which her uncle tells her to go away and play are well portrayed, and there is a realistic picture of the virtuous spinsters, Miss Ainley and Miss Mann, the narrowness of whose lot is neither exaggerated nor cloaked by sentimentality because of their good works. Shirley herself is obviously meant to be the chief exponent of the feminist view, but we cannot help feeling that Charlotte is better at presenting the problem than in finding a solution to it. This is not just because Shirley eventually lapses into conventional marriage; we are not really convinced by the total success of either her marriage or Caroline's, both because of the unhappy marriages we have seen beforehand and because of the unromantic note Charlotte strikes at the end of the book. The real trouble with

Shirley is that she is too good to be true; though her stern treatment of the curates is admirable and she makes a certain number
of witty remarks, for instance that Eve in *Paradise Lost* is modelled
on Milton's cook, much of what she says is embarrassing to read.
The language of Eve's dream reminds us of unreadable Victorian
pseudo-philosophical poems, and even Shirley's adoption of masculine sobriquets like Captain and Esquire seem strained. Charlotte's remark that Shirley was based on Emily in ideal circumstances is a useful indication, since Emily possessed neither health
nor wealth, that Shirley is an unreal character.

There is a fairly obvious link between the feminism and the
perhaps not fully developed theme on which the book opens: the
portrait of Messrs. Donne, Malone, and Sweeting engaged in trivial
gossip when they should be looking after their flock. All three
curates rather fancy themselves as ladies' men; Malone with his
clumsy courtesies to Caroline and Donne with his arrogant courtship of Shirley are obviously totally unsuitable as husbands, and
only the contemptible Sweeting is rewarded with a wife in the
shape of the buxom Dora Sykes. The senior clergymen are not
much better than their curates; the only really virtuous parson in
the book is the saintly if plain Cyril Hall, and he lives happily as
a bachelor with his sister. Clergymen like Malone and Helstone
play an active part in fighting the workers, Donne is anxious to
raise money for not very useful projects in fighting Nonconformity,
and it is left to the women of the district, and perhaps to Mr.
Hall, to do something active in alleviating the hard lot of the
poor.

The clergy thus act as a bridge between the supposedly disparate
public and private themes in *Shirley*.[11] Mr. Helstone is seen as the
most obvious example of a man with many fine qualities but
totally lacking in imagination; as a result he makes a poor clergyman, though he would have made an excellent soldier, being
indeed compared by Shirley to the Duke of Wellington; and he is
totally lacking in sympathy for Caroline's aspirations or for the
grievances of the workers. To a lesser extent, Robert Moore is
presented as a man of bold daring, but one pitiless to those
weaker than himself. Though he is more directly responsible than
Mr. Helstone for ruining the lives of Caroline and the workers,
he is allowed some sympathetic traits, sharing with his brother

Louis a gentle disposition towards animals; he relents towards William Farren, and his conduct towards Caroline is partly excused because of economic necessity. It is economic necessity which turns men like Robert Moore from heroes into hard-faced men, and the war between economic necessity and the creative imagination is the main theme of both the public and private parts of *Shirley*. The conclusion of the book, which sees the fulfilment of Robert Moore's threats to turn the country round Hollow's-mill into an industrial estate, suggests that economic necessity is victorious, although previously Robert's confession to Mr. Yorke about his mercenary proposal to Shirley, his repentance of his harsh conduct to the Luddites, and his marriage to Caroline, would suggest that he is partly redeemed.

The apparent lack of unity in *Shirley* does disappear if we regard both the troubles of the workers and the troubles of Caroline Helstone as originating from the same unfeeling cause. Charlotte had, of course, little insight into what working people were really like, and she treats them with the same distant if benevolent paternalism as the middle-class ladies who try to organise eleemosynary relief for the poor, but this weakness in the exposition of her public theme is made up for by the penetration she displays in charting the hopelessness of Caroline Helstone's position. When she moves away from Caroline to the other three main characters, Charlotte is on less happy ground, but this is the result of two other faults which critics have found in *Shirley*, and of which it is less easy to clear Charlotte.[12]

The third-person narrative results in some obvious clumsinesses, as when the reader is invited to peer over Louis Moore's shoulder as he writes his diary: "Come near, by all means, reader: do not be shy: stoop over his shoulder fearlessly, and read as he scribbles" (S., p. 532). Again, when Caroline Helstone sees Shirley and Robert Moore together and, imagining that they will soon be married, leaves despondently, "The reader is privileged to remain, and try what he can make of the discourse" (S., p. 239). In *Jane Eyre* the narrator, although obviously for the sake of the story not telling us the whole truth, wins our trust, and we proceed quite happily as the mystery unfolds in the same way as it unfolded for the young Jane Eyre. In *Villette* the narrator is dishonest and secretive, and thus reflects the rather unattractive slyness that is part of Lucy Snowe's nature; a dishonest narrator can also make the development of the plot more exciting. But in *Shirley* we have a narrator in whom we are totally uninterested, the autobiographical "I" only appearing in the last pages of the book; and this narrator both earns our distrust by keeping us in the dark about certain incidents and distracts us from seeing events through Caroline Helstone's eyes by inviting us to go behind her back. We are therefore less inclined to be impressed by the more general observations of the narrator, important though these are as expressions of Charlotte's more mature philosophy of realistic pessimism. The beginning of Chapter 7, which describes the illusions of youth, is an impressive example of the philosophy, although at this stage we are probably, as in *Jane Eyre*, still prepared to see the novel after the introductory chapters from Caroline Helstone's point of view.

This expectation receives a rude shock when the focus of the book shifts from Caroline to Shirley. Robert Moore has largely been seen through Caroline's eyes; we know from extra information provided by the narrator that he is in some kind of financial difficulty, but in a way Caroline knows this too, as she must have pondered why the admirable Robert was behaving in such a craven fashion. Shirley, with her disregard of conventionality, is initially seen through the hero-worshipping gaze of Caroline, and we can for a time look up to her too, without asking awkward questions as to why Caroline does not discuss her love for Robert Moore with Shirley, or why Shirley so insensitively appears to encourage Robert and discourage Caroline. But there is then an attempt to develop Shirley as a character in her own right, first through her high-flown speeches and then by the quaint device of Louis Moore's diary; such attempts only serve to turn Shirley into a preposterous figure. Meanwhile, as Robert Moore's conduct is explained by his confession to Mr. Yorke, the virtues of Louis Moore are sung by every character, but his own diary fails to turn him into a convincing or even a likeable human being.

Charlotte Brontë was obviously interested in pitting one character against another: the success of this technique in *Jane Eyre* is clear. She was also interested in exploring the dual nature of a single character; *Villette*, in which there is such an interesting variety of surnames, is perhaps the best place to look for such an exploration. In *Shirley* we feel that Charlotte has in her four main characters tried rather unsuccessfully to combine both techniques. Robert and Louis Moore are brothers, and one can be mistaken for the other. Sometimes, as when Robert is unusually gentle with Caroline, or when Louis attacks Mr. Sympson, we feel that the two brothers have changed roles, and for all the lofty admiration that Louis Moore expresses for Shirley's mind, Mr. Sympson's suspicion that like Robert Moore he was after her money does not seem totally groundless. Charlotte has hardly succeeded in demonstrating through the Moore brothers how a naturally good nature can be warped by business and improved by teaching; most of us prefer Robert for all his honest hardness to the boring and slightly hypocritical Louis.

Although Caroline and Shirley are not related, interestingly the second name of Shirley's father is the same as the maiden name of Caroline's aunt. They also show two sides of the feminist point of view, and again there are times when Caroline displays the boldness of Shirley, and when Shirley is as docile as Caroline. It is not clear how much we are meant to speculate on whether each heroine has married the wrong brother. Caroline is uninterested in Louis: "She acknowledged a steady, manly, kindly air in Louis; but she bent before the secret power of Robert" (S., p. 425). Similarly, Louis sees little in Caroline:

"Caroline, I fancy, is the soul of conscientious punctuality and nice exactitude; she would precisely suit the domestic habits of a certain fastidious kinsman of mine: so delicate, dexterous, quaint, quick, quiet; all done to a minute, all arranged to a strawbreadth: she would suit Robert; but what could *I* do with anything so nearly faultless? *She* is my equal." (S., p. 536)

But this doctrine of the incompatibility of equals and the attraction of opposites does not seem very convincing, partly because the opposite characters are insufficiently differentiated from the similar ones, and partly because in *Villette* Charlotte so magnificently turns the story upside down to show the suitability of a marriage of like with like. The prospect of the marriage of Robert Moore and Shirley is much more before the reader's eyes than any match between Louis and Caroline, and we are presumably meant to feel it unsuitable because we see it causing distress to Caroline, and because Shirley's fortune brings out the businessman in Robert. Nevertheless it would seem that the two, to use a favourite word of Charlotte's, "suited" each other magnificently, and a marriage between Robert Moore and Shirley would have seemed to signify a much more positive victory for the feminist forces of imagination against hard-headed reason; presumably Charlotte's pessimism got the better of her here.

As some compensation for the weakness of the Moore brothers and Shirley, the minor characters in the novel are good portraits, and show Charlotte's ability to paint on a wider canvas than that which she used in *Villette* or *Jane Eyre*. The excellent and economical sketches of the three curates and the Yorke family have perhaps not been fully appreciated, either because readers have not been able to see their significance in the novel, or because they have been distracted by the obvious biographical parallels. It is of course true that in writing about the clergy and in writing about a middle-class Yorkshire family, Charlotte was writing from her own experiences, and that she is less successful when she moves away from these experiences. The workers are not portrayed at all, and the upper classes as represented by the Sympsons and Sir Philip Nunnely are caricatures. Nevertheless it would be true to say that whereas in *Villette* and *Jane Eyre* the intensity of focus on the heroine and a few central characters prevents us from gaining a satisfactory portrait of people like Père Silas and Mrs. Fairfax, in *Shirley* it is characters in this middle range who do something to make up for the deficiencies in the main characters.

The same question mark hangs over *Shirley* as hangs over *The Professor* and Anne Brontë's works. It is doubtful whether they would be read in their own right were it not for the greatness of the novels with which they are obviously associated. Certainly for students of *Jane Eyre* and *Villette*, *Shirley* has great interest; we can see the author experimenting with and changing her narrative method and exploring the concept of dual personality, while hardening her philosophy of life into a mood of sombre pessimism. For the student of the history of ideas, too, *Shirley* must be interesting not so much for anything very profound that it has to say on the position of women or the position of the working classes as for the parallels between the two themes that it attempts to draw. Nevertheless as a novel *Shirley* cannot be considered to be in the same class as either *Jane Eyre* or *Villette*; if it lacks some of the apparently glaring faults of both these works, it has none of their magnificent virtues either.

TEN

Villette

By the time *Villette* was written, something of Charlotte's tragic story was known to the literary critics of the day. Though there were still attacks on the book's coarseness, and though Matthew Arnold found the book disagreeable because it was full of hunger, rebellion, and rage, most contemporary reviewers were disposed to be lenient.[1] After the publication of Mrs. Gaskell's biography, the links between *Villette* and Charlotte's own experiences were so obvious, even though the Heger story could only be guessed at, that the biographical school of criticism more or less took over the novel. The biographical interest of the book has no doubt been its main attraction for the general reader, since Lucy Snowe is undoubtedly a less attractive heroine than Jane Eyre, her adventures are less exciting, and as a story *Villette* contains even more apparent flaws of design than *Jane Eyre*. Not until very recently has the possible greatness and undoubted originality of *Villette* been suggested, and the distractions of biographical parallels and narrative faults, as well as the fact that *Villette* is not a well-known novel, will probably always prevent it from achieving proper recognition.[2]

Most people who read *Villette* for the first time probably feel the slight disappointment that Charlotte's publishers felt at the unexpected turn the story takes. The publishing history of *Villette* is a complicated one.[3] In 1850, Charlotte was busy preparing a second edition of her sister's novels and revising *The Professor* for possible publication. She abandoned the latter project early in 1851, and then presumably began *Villette*, although grave ill health in 1851 prevented her from achieving much in that year. By the spring of 1852 she had recovered and wrote with such application that she was able to send two volumes to Smith and Elder in October, and the third in November. *Villette* was published at the end of January 1853.

It has been suggested that one reason for the reservations that George Smith had about *Villette* was that he saw himself portrayed as Dr. John and his mother as Mrs. Bretton. Charlotte's relations with her publisher were strange, and it is unfortunate that we do not have the full correspondence between the two.[4] Nevertheless it seems inherently improbable that Charlotte should have risked portraying George Smith first as an attractive hero with whom a governess very like herself falls in love, and then as a character somehow inferior to the far from prepossessing Paul Emanuel. The relationship between Charlotte and George Smith was a sufficiently businesslike one to make her mind that he did not pay her more money for *Villette*, and it hardly seems likely that she would want to strain such a relationship by painting him in such a revealing and ultimately uncomplimentary light. Like George Smith, Dr. John is cheerful and able to mitigate Lucy Snowe's solitude in the same way that George Smith tried to introduce his shy author to the literary world; the resemblance does not appear to go a great deal further.

The biographical critics want to have things all their own way because in addition to postulating a love affair between George Smith and Charlotte, for which there is no evidence, as a basis for the first part of the novel, they want to make Charlotte's more certain love for Monsieur Heger the starting point of the second half. It is true that *Villette* is in some ways both a reflection of Charlotte's immense loneliness in the dreary winter of 1852 and a re-creation of her experiences in Belgium nine years before, with loneliness rather than love the predominating theme. On the other hand, as in *The Professor*, it is a great mistake to look for exact parallels; Monsieur Heger appears from all accounts to have been neither as irascible nor as unattractive as Paul Emanuel. A possible model for the more repellent side of Paul Emanuel is James Taylor, who proposed marriage to Charlotte in 1851; he then left for India, a reminder of Paul Emanuel's journey to the West Indies, and sent letters to Charlotte which eventually ceased, a reminder of Dr. John. This dual role is perhaps a reason why those who seek exact parallels have never given James Taylor his due when seeking models for *Villette*; Charlotte's willingness to allow reality to suggest but not to dictate is more in evidence if we look at James Taylor than if we look at Monsieur Heger or George Smith.

As with so many Brontë novels, the supposed autobiographical element is used as an excuse for supposed structural flaws. The replacement of one hero by another is a strange device, but it is explained by Charlotte having two loves in her life, although of course in no sense did Monsieur Heger replace George Smith. The episodic nature of the book with its apparent false starts with the Brettons and with Miss Marchmont is explained by Charlotte's wish to chronicle the story of her life, although there is no parallel in this story for Lucy Snowe's stay in Bretton or her year with Miss Marchmont. The strange coincidences which stand out in the novel even more jarringly than in *Jane Eyre* are less easy to explain on these lines. Lucy Snowe is amazingly lucky to find a job at Madame Beck's school and amazingly lucky when she collapses to be rescued by the only friends she has; Charlotte Brontë's journey to Brussels was carefully planned, and although she did visit the confessional as Lucy Snowe did, she was not so lucky as to find any friends thereafter. On the other hand the lack of incident in the novel, which makes it seem so sombre after the excitements of *Jane Eyre*, is explained by Charlotte's wish to paint a realistic portrait of her own dreary life. If we say that Charlotte was not writing an autobiographical novel, *Villette* does seem a little exposed to these criticisms.

Villette opens with an account by Lucy Snowe of her stay at the house of the Brettons. The even tenor of this household is disturbed by the arrival of a small child, Polly Home, who at first misses her widowed father, but finds compensation in the presence of John Bretton, the cheerfully extrovert son of Lucy's godmother, Mrs. Bretton. Lucy plays only a spectator's part in narrating these events, and we are ill prepared for the sudden switch of focus to Lucy herself, as she describes first in vague terms some disaster to her family; her stay as a paid companion to Miss Marchmont, an elderly spinster whose lover had died in an accident just before the wedding; and then on Miss Marchmont's death her sudden decision to go to Brussels. Lucy's voyage to Brussels and the misfortunes that she meets are described in graphic detail which even in these days of easy travel abroad arouse a sympathetic chord from the traveller. On her arrival in Brussels, after temporarily losing her trunk she is rescued by a kindly fellow Englishman, loses her way again, meets two insulting Belgians, and eventually by a stroke of good fortune arrives at the school of Madame Beck, at which one of her fellow travellers on the boat to Belgium, Ginevra Fanshawe, is a pupil. The slight acquaintance with Ginevra gives Lucy Snowe sufficient courage to ask for a post with Madame Beck; it so happens that Madame Beck is dissatisfied with the drunken Irish lady whose job it is to teach English to her children, and after seeking the advice of her cousin Paul Emanuel, Madame Beck employs Lucy, though she makes doubly sure by carefully examining her belongings while Lucy pretends to be asleep.

Lucy is soon promoted to being a regular teacher at the school, where in a scene very similar to that in *The Professor* she establishes her authority over some recalcitrant pupils. She comes into contact again with Ginevra Fanshawe, who boasts to her of her two lovers, Colonel de Hamal and "Isidore." The latter is eventually revealed to be Dr. John, a physician who has come to attend the Beck children when they are ill. Dr. John's regular appearances at the school make Lucy initially suspect that there is a love affair between him and Madame Beck, and then after a curious incident in which Lucy sees two letters dropped from a window of the adjacent boys' school she thinks he is in love with Rosine, the portress. The truth is eventually revealed when Lucy is persuaded by Paul Emanuel to take a man's part in a play on Madame Beck's birthday; and playing opposite Ginevra Fanshawe, she notices that her smiles and glances are directed towards Dr. John. After these excitements the school breaks up for the long vacation, during which Lucy is seized by a dreadful depression. Wandering through Brussels in this state she visits a Roman Catholic confessional and on coming out of it collapses. Recovering from her faint she discovers herself among the familiar furniture of the Bretton household; it turns out to be John Bretton who has rescued her, and, as Lucy confesses she had realised, John Bretton is no other than Dr. John, who, as if Charlotte was determined to have as many coincidences as possible, is also the person who rescued Lucy on her first arrival in Brussels.

Lucy stays some time with the Brettons at their house, La Terrasse, and discusses Ginevra Fanshawe with John Bretton. She visits an art gallery, and is struck by a portrait of Cleopatra; Paul Emanuel, Alfred de Hamal, and Dr. John all react to this picture in different ways. The Brettons and Lucy also go to a concert, where Paul Emanuel is again shocked by Lucy's appearance in a pink dress, and Dr. John learns the true worth of Ginevra when he sees her sneering at his mother. Term then begins and Lucy is unhappy to leave the Brettons, but Dr. John sends her a kind letter which she takes up into the garret to read, and there sees the figure of the nun whose ghost is supposed to haunt the school. Dr. John, who happens to be visiting Lucy, reassures her, restores her letter, which in her panic she has lost, and continues to write to her. He also takes her to the theatre to see the famous actress Vashti, whose impassioned acting moves and horrifies Lucy, though it hardly affects the cool Dr. John. Fire breaks out at the theatre: there is a slight panic, and Dr. John is able to rescue a young girl, who turns out eventually to be Polly Home. But this revelation does not come for several weeks, during which Lucy receives no more letters from Dr. John: Ginevra Fanshawe explains that the girl rescued is the daughter of her uncle, the Count de Bassompierre, and it is as Paulina Mary Home de Bassompierre that this girl introduces herself to Lucy when she is eventually invited by Mrs. Bretton to La Terrasse.

Lucy now has two sets of friends, but as she is troubled by the thought that both Madame Beck and Paul Emanuel are reading her letters she buries them under the pear tree in the garden, and again sees the nun. After a public lecture by Paul Emanuel there is a party at the Hotel Crécy at which it becomes obvious that Dr. John has transferred his affections from Ginevra to Paulina. Monsieur Paul is at first rude to Lucy, but later apologises, and she is surprised by his sudden change to mildness both on this occasion and later when she accidentally breaks his spectacles. On Monsieur Paul's birthday Lucy pretends she has no present for him, and is treated to a tirade on the perfidy of the English, to which she gives a spirited reply, but on finding him inspecting her desk she makes up her quarrel, and the reader is then treated to a chapter on his virtues as a teacher, although being taught by Monsieur Paul is not without its difficulties, as Lucy discovers when she takes lessons from him. Lucy realises her love for Dr. John is as buried as her letters and forms ambitions to start a school of her own; while pondering on this in the garden in the company of Monsieur Paul she sees the nun again.

On meeting Paulina, who has been travelling in France, Lucy learns that she is in love with John Bretton. Monsieur Paul takes the school for a picnic in the country, and treats Lucy with gentle consideration, although in the evening when he comes to the school to ask for her Lucy perversely pretends to have gone to bed. Madame Beck sends Lucy into the old city, where she meets a hideous old lady, Madame Walravens, and an old priest, Père Silas. The latter, who happens to be the priest whom Lucy had approached in the confessional, explains that he and Madame Walravens are kept by the charity of Paul Emanuel, who had been in love with Madame Walravens's granddaughter. Madame Beck laughs at the bad reception Lucy has received from Madame Walravens, and tells Lucy to forget Paul Emanuel, with his heavy responsibilities. Lucy cannot do this, and the bond between the two is further strengthened when Lucy is examined by two professors who believe that the work Monsieur Paul is exhibiting as Lucy's own was written by himself. The examination goes badly until Lucy realises that the two professors are the two men who had insulted her on her first arrival in Villette, and writes an essay on "Human Justice" full of passion inspired by this coincidence. However, not only Madame Beck but also the dead weight of Roman Catholicism hinders the love between Paul and Lucy, whereas the love affair between John Bretton and Paulina prospers; after initial objections, Paulina's father gives his consent to their marriage, and Lucy unveils their happy future life.

Madame Beck announces Monsieur Paul's impending departure to the West Indies, and tries to prevent Lucy from saying goodbye to him, but Lucy speaks harshly to her, accusing her of being a dog in the manger. A sleeping draught which Lucy takes does not work, and she walks out into the night to find Villette in full festival. She sees the de Bassompierres and Brettons, the Becks, Père Silas and Madame Walravens. She overhears the conversation of the latter party. There is talk of Justine Mary, the name of Monsieur Paul's former love, but the Justine Mary who arrives is just an ordinary Belgian girl. There is talk of her impending marriage to one of the party, and Lucy thinks that this must be Monsieur Paul himself, especially because when he arrives he engages in brilliant banter with Justine Mary and announces that he has deferred his departure for a fortnight until he has completed a certain piece of business. Lucy leaves, sees a carriage from which someone waves to her, and on arriving back at the school thinks she sees the nun, but this turns out to be a bolster dressed in a long black stole.

In the morning it is revealed that Ginevra Fanshawe has eloped with Colonel de Hamal; it was she who had waved to Lucy, and it was de Hamal who had used the nun as a convenient disguise. Ginevra's future life is briefly summarised; Colonel de Hamal is not an ideal husband, but Ginevra, an excellent portrait of trivial selfishness, manages to survive fairly well. Lucy still waits in suspense for some word from Monsieur Paul, hoping that her conjectures on the night of the festival have proved false. Her hopes are not in vain, for Monsieur Paul appears, speaks abruptly to Madame Beck, and takes Lucy for a walk. On the walk he reveals to her that the business which had caused him to defer his departure had been the setting up of a school for Lucy, which he shows to her. He also reveals his love for Lucy: "Lucy, take my love. One day share my life. Be my dearest, first on earth" (V., p. 589).

Monsieur Paul departs. Lucy's school succeeds, and after three years Monsieur Paul is ready to return; in an ambiguous ending which hints at his death by shipwreck, Charlotte refuses to conclude with the conventional wedding and invites her readers to "picture union and a happy succeeding life." As in *Jane Eyre*, where she ends not with the happy, fulfilled life on earth of the Rochesters but with St. John Rivers striving for the heavenly crown, so in *Villette* Charlotte perversely reverses the picture. The last words of the novel are: "Madame Beck prospered all the days of her life; so did Père Silas; Madame Walravens fulfilled her ninetieth year before she died. Farewell."

Perversity would at first sight seem the key note to *Villette*.[5] Few readers approaching the novel for the first time cannot have felt both surprise and irritation when the eccentric Paul Emanuel

begins to replace the conventional John Bretton as the novel's
hero. This surprise and irritation are increased when we consider
what appears to be the false start of the book in Bretton; there is
little to prepare us for Paul Emanuel here. The episode of Miss
Marchmont is isolated from the rest of the novel, and it is not
until *Villette* ends that we see the connection between Miss
Marchmont's unhappy lot and the fate of Lucy Snowe. The coincidences in this book are perhaps more conspicuous than those
in *Jane Eyre*; obviously for the sake of the plot Lucy has to meet
John Bretton and Polly Home again, but in making John Bretton
Ginevra Fanshawe's admirer and Polly Home her cousin, in causing Lucy to arrive at Madame Beck's door in the first place and in
causing her to visit Père Silas, so closely connected with Paul
Emanuel, in the confessional, Charlotte Brontë is surely being too
economical in her characters. Lucy Snowe's slyness in admitting to
these coincidences may make them less glaring, although it makes
the plot more confusing, but her dishonesty as a narrator makes
her an unattractive figure, and we are less sympathetic to her
adventures—which are in truth fairly ordinary—and less sympathetic to the abstract generalisations or frissons of romantic
horror in which she indulges when the action seems at a standstill.

These objections explain why the book has never been popular,
but they can be shown to be fairly superficial. Of course it is surprising when John Bretton begins to lose his role as hero in the
novel, but we should have been prepared for this. The first section
of the novel, so far from being a false start, shows John Bretton
involved with Polly Home, not Lucy Snowe, and treating her with
that self-satisfied indifference to her feelings for him which he later
inflicts on the unfortunate Lucy. When she meets him again in
Villette after she has lost her baggage, John Bretton is kind to
Lucy, but his kindness is not sufficient to prevent her getting lost
again. At Madame Beck's Lucy imagines John to be in love with
Madame Beck and Rosine the portress; in fact he is in love with
the equally worthless Ginevra Fanshawe. In hoping that her own
charms will somehow prove superior, Lucy Snowe is obviously
appealing to imagination rather than reason, and as she frequently
makes clear, both explicitly and implicitly by using the image of
the nun and the moon to stand for delusive imagination, the
whole of *Villette* is concerned to show that we cannot live in a

dream world. It is of course a barrier between John Bretton and Lucy Snowe that he is so lacking in imagination and feeling; he is, for instance, almost unmoved by the brilliance and horror of Vashti's acting. His solid British good sense, to which his surname gives the clue, is instrumental in rescuing Lucy from the unreal world of loneliness, even though she temporarily falls into an unreal dependence on his letters, compared in a rather peculiar fashion to the Rhine, Nile, and Ganges.[6] The mirage of John Bretton's love is of course a necessary stage in Lucy's progress to reality, just as acquaintance with Lucy is a means of leading John away from the sirenlike attraction of Ginevra Fanshawe to the more solid worth of Polly Home.

Polly is not a very solid character, although the novel begins by focussing on her as a child, lonely and dependent on John Bretton's casual affection. This mirrors Lucy's position, and the first three chapters also have the advantage of showing Lucy as a colourless observer; her emergence from this position into a life of her own is a surprise, but it is what gives the novel point. Lucy gains a life of her own by going out into the world, and we feel that when she re-enters the Bretton menage after her collapse she is in danger of becoming a cipher again. As it is, the fortunate rescue of Polly at the theatre resolves the situation, and it is Polly because she retains certain childlike qualities who seems more of a cipher. The courtship of Polly and John Bretton is a peculiar one; we see it at a distance initially through the spiteful eyes of Ginevra Fanshawe, then through the presumably slightly jealous observation of Lucy herself. The initial hostility of Polly's father to John seems more than normal parental jealousy. It is at this stage that Lucy is most explicit in the reservations she has about Dr. John, drawing attention to his guile and his faults, and even the prosperity outlined for the young couple has an ambiguous ring about it, since the novel ends with the prosperity of those who have separated Lucy and Paul.

Polly is called Paulina when she reappears later in the novel, and this change of name taken in conjunction with John Graham Bretton's two Christian names may provide the clue to the slight unease we feel about this couple. In writing about Dr. John, the helper of the distressed and the healer of the poor, Charlotte is anxious to paint a portrait of a hero with solid British virtues and few faults who, like William Crimsworth, wins his way to prosperity and a charming wife, Paulina de Bassompierre, whose idealistic conversations with Lucy Snowe are meant to be admired. Both portraits are, like those of the average Victorian hero and heroine, a little dull. But Charlotte is also writing about the selfish and insensitive Graham, whose vanity is tickled by winning the affection of a slightly pettish child wife, Polly Home, and such a relationship implying male superiority and female subservience is one which Charlotte is anxious to reject. Of course the division between the two sides of each character is not a rigid one, any more than Charlotte is rigorous in her use of the various names, although there is one passage where after speaking of Paulina's highmindedness she explicitly says, "she looked and spoke—the little Polly of Bretton—petulant, sensitive" (V., p. 444). But Charlotte is always ready to look on both sides of the coin, and some of the difficulties we experience in ar.alysing both Paulina and John Bretton arise from the fact that we are meant simultaneously to be both approving and disapproving of conventional romantic love.

John Bretton first appears in the book after some mystery involving yet another name, Isidore, as the lover of Ginevra Fanshawe, one of Charlotte's most convincing characters who serves a multitude of purposes. Paulina Home is meant to be her superior, and yet the two cousins, both the daughters of widowers, have a certain amount in common. It is easy to imagine the young Polly turning into Ginevra, and even when she has grown out of her childish petulance she retains the doll-like charm which both attracts and repels Lucy. It is difficult to steer a middle course between the school of criticism which attributes lesbian leanings to Charlotte without any difficulty and a more old-fashioned view which would find it repellent to imagine Charlotte describing one woman being sexually attracted by another. Yet it would seem that some of the latent hostility to John Bretton can be explained by the fact that Lucy is actually jealous of the hold he has over both Ginevra and Paulina. Certainly we can say that *Villette* is a novel in which ordinary sexual love receives short shrift.

Two rather baffling scenes make this point clear. The first occurs when Lucy at short notice is suddenly called upon to act a male part in the fête for Madame Beck's birthday.[7] Paul Emanuel, who certainly plays a larger and better part in the earlier part of the story than Lucy Snowe or most readers give him credit for, insists that Lucy should play, initially requests that Lucy should dress as a man, and then accepts her semi-masculine costume. Lucy's behaviour in first refusing to wear male clothes, then acting her part as Ginevra Fanshawe's lover with great passion, is more baffling. Her reluctance to dress as a man could be taken as an assertion of her own femininity, but Lucy does not seem a very feminine character, and the dress she is wearing even before she adapts it for the sake of the vaudeville is hardly a feminine one; indeed her later attempts to introduce a little colour into her life by wearing a pink dress to go to the concert win the contempt of Monsieur Paul. In any case, though she begins the play still dressed partly as a woman, she is soon moved by the presence of Dr. John in the audience and the subconscious realisation that he is in love with Ginevra to adopt an aggressively masculine role. "In the 'Ours' [French for "bear"], or sincere lover, I saw Dr. John. Did I pity him, as erst? No, I hardened my heart, rivalled and out-rivalled him. I knew myself but a fop, but where *he* was outcast *I* could please" (V., p. 164).

The sexual ambiguities here are clear. Lucy is meant to be acting the part of a fop, like Alfred de Hamal, but so moulds her performance that she behaves like a more charming version of Dr. John, who is several times in the book compared to a bear. Having initially been reluctant to play the part of a man Lucy now tries both to be and to be better than Dr. John. At one level Lucy could be trying to help Dr. John, to show him that in order to win Ginevra, he must show something of de Hamal's airs and graces, although she has not yet realised that Dr. John is Isidore. More obviously Lucy does seem to be trying to win Ginevra, even if she is only play acting, from both de Hamal and Dr. John. Lucy's contempt for the play and for its chief advocates like Zélie St. Pierre, who had insisted that she should dress as a man, is obvious; and this contempt appears to show a deeper dislike of the insincere masquerade into which the normal courtship of men and women appeared in Charlotte's eyes to have fallen. Zélie St. Pierre had once thought she might be able to marry Paul Emanuel, and her anxiety about Lucy's clothes might appear to show that she regarded Lucy as a rival, but what the whole scene seems to show is that Charlotte despised such rivalries.

The chapter entitled "The Cleopatra" is even more peculiar. The *Cleopatra* is a portrait of which Rubens might well be the painter: her vast size, indolent posture, insufficient clothing, and general untidiness are all commented upon unfavourably by Lucy Snowe. Paul Emanuel is deeply shocked that Lucy should have been allowed to look at the picture, which he himself admires and studies for some time. Alfred de Hamal is equally taken by Cleopatra, although his attitude is more frivolous, while John Graham passes fairly quickly by the portrait, at which he casts a fastidious glance. At this stage in the book Lucy admires Dr. John, and she thinks almost as badly of Paul Emanuel as she does of Alfred de Hamal. It would seem then that Dr. John's attitude is to be praised while the prudery and the prurience of the other two men is to be condemned. This explanation of the chapter would seem to fit in with the idea that *Villette* is not enthusiastic about normal sexuality, but this is difficult to maintain in view of Dr. John's role as a proponent of normal sexuality both in the rest of the book and in this chapter, which he ends with the significant words, "Compare that mulatto with Ginevra" (V., p. 243). Nor is it easy to see why Paul Emanuel is exposed in such a poor light during this chapter, although it is true that Charlotte through him attacks French furtive immorality as opposed to British straightforwardness.

Paul is shocked that Lucy should have been allowed to see the picture; she does not like the picture, and in a sense his anxiety about her welfare contrasts favourably with the carelessness of Dr. John. On the other hand Paul is obviously at fault in insisting that Lucy should be looking at the four pictures entitled *La Vie d'une Femme*. These pictures are in Lucy's eyes as ugly aesthetically as the *Cleopatra*, but presumably she has moral objections to both kinds of picture as well. At first sight the moral antithesis is between moral decadence represented by Cleopatra and conventional decorum represented by Paul Emanuel's choice, with Lucy Snowe and presumably Dr. John as well disliking either extreme. But the four portraits in *La Vie d'une Femme* are not really decorous, although they may be conventional. They are associated with religion; all but the Jeune Mère have some religious symbol in the picture, and even the Jeune Mère is an ugly parody of the Madonna. They are associated with a view that woman's primary role is that of wife and mother; even the Jeune Fille who looks so well behaved is obviously a hypocrite and is thinking worldly thoughts when she is pretending to think of church. Thus in despising the *Cleopatra* and *La Vie d'une Femme* Lucy Snowe appears to be despising coarse female sensuality and the way that convention channels this sensuality into producing women who are "bloodless, brainless nonentities" (V., p. 238).

Paul Emanuel's preference for *La Vie d'une Femme*, and his lengthy inspection of the *Cleopatra* are difficult to explain. We can of course say that his taste has been warped by his French Catholic upbringing, and in a sense he is bound to appear in an inferior light to John Bretton when he is standing for French Catholicism against British Protestantism, although Charlotte does see the shortcomings of British sangfroid when she shows John Bretton unmoved by Vashti. We can also declare that Charlotte's aim is to make Paul Emanuel improve in the novel, as he becomes subject to Lucy's influence; it is not just that he improves in Lucy's eyes. He is described in this chapter as despotic; when Lucy returns to the school his habits are described as "unwarrantably interfering," and he is summed up as "not at all a good, little man, though he had good points," and this chapter ends with the remarkable sentence: "Really that little man was dreadful: a mere sprite of caprice and ubiquity: one never knew either his whim or his whereabout" (V., p. 287).

Paul's spying habits, which he shares with Madame Beck, are presumably another feature of his Catholic upbringing, although because he is more open in his raids on Lucy's desk his behaviour is more acceptable. His interference and his tyrannical behaviour can with hindsight be explained by his genuine interest in Lucy and anxiety to do his best for her; by contrast John Bretton does not interfere enough, and is too ready, except in a crisis, to let circumstances determine his actions, as is shown by his courtship of Ginevra.

The metamorphosis of Paul Emanuel from the waspish despot through the lovable if authoritarian teacher into the real love of Lucy's life is a remarkable artistic achievement. The first time we read *Villette* we are surprised at the change; it begins in the chapters when Lucy realises that her love for John Bretton will lead nowhere, and we and she are so preoccupied with this old love that we do not see the new love approaching. Monsieur Paul's jealous behaviour at the Hotel Crécy seems a comic irritant, and we do not contrast it favourably with Dr. John's indifference. Lucy says that "Professor Paul Emanuel . . . never lost an opportunity of intimating his opinion that mine was rather a fiery and rash nature—adventurous, indocile, and audacious" (V., p. 359), but in fact Paul has penetrated to the dangerous passion hidden behind Lucy's prim exterior, whereas a few pages later (V., p. 379) Lucy realises Dr. John's "entire misapprehension of my character and nature. He wanted always to give me a role not mine." At this stage in the book we can see that Paul has improved slightly in Lucy's eyes; his speech at the Hotel Crécy is highly praised, and even when in the previous chapter he quarrels with Lucy for visiting the de Bassompierres, his character is described in terms significantly better than the previous summing up, "Never was a better little man, in some points, than Monsieur Paul; never, in others, a more waspish little despot" (V., p. 361). This improvement does not perhaps quite prepare us for the complete change into the beloved master of the final chapters, but even this change is difficult to fault.

In rereading *Mansfield Park* most readers cannot help hoping that the weddings to which the book seems to be leading up, those between Fanny Price and Henry Crawford, and Mary Crawford and Edmund Bartram, will by some miracle take place, and that the disastrous disgrace of the Crawfords and boring marriage between Fanny and Edmund will be averted. In rereading *Villette* we do not hope that Lucy will marry John Bretton, and when Paul Emanuel appears to be occupying more and more of the stage we do not, as we probably do on our first acquaintance with the novel, regard him as an intrusion. The love between Lucy and Paul is based on mutual respect for the other person's intellectual powers; they share a passionate regard for justice, both have a vivid imagination (Monsieur Paul believes in the nun), but believe that the imagination must not be allowed free rein. Their common interest in teaching is sufficient to overcome Paul's Catholic and Gallic prejudices on the one hand, and Lucy's dangerous leanings towards romanticism on the other. As in *Jane Eyre*, where Jane is initially too subservient and Rochester too masterful, Lucy and Paul are initially not suited to each other, but each learns from the other as the novel progresses. Monsieur Paul becomes kindlier and more tactful; his preparation of a school for Lucy is cunningly contrived, and is surprising from a man whom Lucy has characterised as a bungling schemer. Lucy learns to be more honest, and to live less in a world of her own; her love for John Bretton is bottled up in her head (the metaphor is not inappropriate in view of what Lucy does to John's letters) in such a way that even Paul Emanuel cannot appreciate its strength, whereas even the unfriendly Madame Beck can see and try to thwart Lucy's love for Paul.

Monsieur Paul emerges from the book as an admirable character. His first recommendations to Madame Beck that she should employ Lucy and his insistence that Lucy should act a part in the play are both instrumental in and symbolic of the breaking down of the barriers which Lucy has put between herself and the world. The first chapters of the novel show Lucy in the unattractive role of a mere spectator of events, and are important for this reason. The episode with Miss Marchmont not only prepares us for Lucy's eventual suffering, but also shows us the danger Lucy is in of retreating completely from her destiny:

I had wanted to compromise with Fate: to escape occasional great agonies by submitting to a whole life of privations and small pains. Fate would not so be pacified; nor would Providence sanction this shrinking sloth and cowardly indolence. (V., p. 40)

Fate is a key word in the novel,[8] and it can be used to excuse the coincidences in the book which, together with Lucy's reluctance to admit them, have been attacked by many readers. Fate is driving Lucy back to the Brettons, where she will almost break her heart because of John Graham's neglect: her refusal to admit that she has recognised him is part of her unwillingness to accept her destiny, an unwillingness that is both cowardly and heroic. Fate is also leading Lucy to Paul Emanuel; her reluctance to acknowledge that Paul is interested in her, as in her delayed admission that it is he who has given her the violets, is caused by her infatuation with John Graham, which in its turn is due to her inability to see what her allotted role is.

Where fate is leading Lucy Snowe is where it had led Miss Marchmont, a long lonely life with only the memories of a love blighted just before it came to fruition. The ending of the novel is, apparently at Mr. Brontë's request, a little ambiguous, and perhaps this note of ambiguity is desirable, as throughout the novel Charlotte, ringing the changes on Lucy as a young woman and Lucy as a white-haired old woman, matured and embittered by experiences, gives us contradictory views on almost everything. We have seen that both John Graham, Polly Hume, and Paul Emanuel are judged very differently at different stages in the novel; even Ginevra Fanshawe and Madame Beck, fairly straightforward portraits of selfishness and slyness, are at times praised. Nor does Lucy, any more than some modern critics of *Villette*,[9] seem able to make up her mind about the conflicting claims of Reason or Imagination, or on a whole range of social, religious, and educational issues. These uncertainties make Lucy Snowe a much less attractive figure than Jane Eyre, as Charlotte undoubtedly intended, and at times it seems as if Charlotte's other avowed intention of teasing and disappointing[10] the reader by constantly taking him down blind alleys has got the better of her, and that the only certainty in the novel is that nothing is certain.

This chief ambiguity to which the final ambiguity points is reminiscent of *Wuthering Heights*. There are other features, too, in *Villette* to remind us of Emily's novel. It is possible to compare John Graham's superficial handsomeness and charm with the character of Edgar Linton, and even to see something of Heathcliff in Paul Emanuel, who has an unattractive exterior, but has genuine spiritual affinities with Lucy. It is more usual to say that in *Villette* Charlotte harks back to her early Angrian works,[11] but it is in *Wuthering Heights* rather than in the Angrian tales that we find the tension between total surrender to the imagination and the harsh claims of reality which *Villette* reflects so well. Both novels seem to find an almost sinister delight in recounting details of physical and mental anguish; occasionally they become almost ludicrous, as when Lucy explains how she used to cut her fingers when sharpening her pencil. In both novels the narrative method is unusual and effective: the shuttling to and fro between past and present, between the detached Lockwood and the involved Nelly Dean in Emily's work can be compared fairly to Charlotte's constant shifts between the mature and the young Lucy Snowe. In both novels we feel the presence of the author in addition to the two main narrators, and the fact that the author, though elusive, seems to disapprove of the judgements of the two narrators, because they are insufficiently involved in the events they describe, is an additional common feature. Between writing *Shirley* and *Villette*, Charlotte was involved in revising *Wuthering Heights*, and though Charlotte's earlier works contain experiments with different levels of narrative and various kinds of ambivalence, it looks as if the controlled ambiguities of *Villette* owe something to this revision. Although it has taken longer for *Villette* than for *Wuthering Heights* to escape from the charges of wild incoherence and though it is still handicapped, unlike Emily's novel, by the attention of biographers, it is now true that critics of the Brontës are beginning to see both novels as works of immense power, although they are still in difficulties about how to interpret them.

The main difference between the two books is that whereas Lockwood and Nelly Dean are largely commenting on people very different from themselves, a great deal of Lucy Snowe's commentary is about Lucy Snowe, and therefore, instead of the contrast between the savage and extraordinary events in *Wuthering Heights* and their humdrum narrators, we have a distinction in *Villette* between the life of stifling ordinariness which Lucy leads and the exceptional richness of her inner life. In her desire to give Lucy a realistic background, Charlotte succeeds much better than in her other novels and much better than Emily in creating a rich range of minor characters. Zélie St. Pierre is a masterly portrait of an acidulated schoolmistress, and the claustrophobic atmosphere which pervades even the best of schools is brilliantly evoked in *Villette*. But it would be a mistake to reduce *Villette* to a sociological documentary, or even a feminist tract, through writers interested in feminism have rightly concentrated their attention on this novel in preference to other works of Charlotte.

As a realistic novel and as a piece of propaganda *Villette* is weakened by Lucy's unreliability as a narrator and her unashamed though uncertain bias as an advocate for British Protestantism against foreign Catholicism.[12] Nor do the most memorable parts of the novel, Lucy's departure from London, her loneliness in the long vacation, and her final somnambulist vision of Villette, have anything to do with *Villette*'s value as a documentary novel. These scenes are designed to show, and succeed in showing, the force of the imagination which can pervade even the most unpromising lives. It is Charlotte's great achievement in *Villette* that she can make the realistic descriptions more interesting and the imaginative visions more convincing by the interplay between the two. John Graham is responsible for many of Lucy's fondest dreams, but he is an ordinary phlegmatic man at heart. Paul Emanuel plays a large part in Lucy's ordinary life at the school, but it is he who has the vision to inspire and to match Lucy's true worth. At the beginning Lucy is ill prepared to give rein to her imagination; by the end of the book, and at various points in it when the elderly Lucy comments on the immature Lucy's delusions, it would seem that the imagination is condemned; and yet on balance *Villette* would seem to be full of tributes to the imagination, provided that it is controlled.

Imagination and control are the two most precious gifts of the novelist, and, as some critics but not many biographers have appreciated,[13] *Villette* is not Charlotte's record of her life in Belgium but a spiritual autobiography of her dilemma as a writer. Her dilemma is that of the novelist, committed to a realist mode and a temporal process, who wants to make a timeless moral point. Most readers of the Brontës' novels, distracted by biography, by those who have exaggerated the importance of Angria, by popular prejudice and by superficial flaws of a fairly elementary nature, have assumed that they did give way to their imaginations too freely and did not exercise sufficient control. *Villette* takes up this challenge and gives the answer to it.

Conclusion

~

While critics and biographers fight over the Brontë sisters, literary historians have been baffled by them. Isolated by poverty from the books their contemporaries read, and deriving much of their inspiration from foreign sources and the books of an earlier generation, the Brontës are difficult to fit into the tradition of the nineteenth-century realist novel. This difficulty has caused some critics to throw over the traces, and to consider the Brontës without any reference to their nineteenth-century background, while others, anxious to place the Brontës more accurately, have fitted them rather unfairly in the category of books which George Eliot described as "Silly Novels by Lady Novelists."

It is important to remember that the Brontës were novelists of the 1840s, sharing many of the preoccupations of their great contemporaries, even though their isolation caused them to show their preoccupations in a startlingly original way. In their experiments with different levels of narrative, in their exploration of dual personalities, and in their refusal to be tied down by conventional realism, the Brontës do remind us of their eighteenth-century predecessors as well as twentieth-century innovators in the novel. Some of the novels appear to be marred by clumsy plotting, a reliance on coincidence, and the trappings of Victorian melodrama, but these faults must not be used as an excuse for dragging the Brontës down to the level of the ephemeral escapist fiction which flourished in the middle of Victoria's reign.

It is inevitable that the closest parallels to and best commentaries on the Brontës' novels are the other Brontë novels. Even if we did not have evidence for their close collaboration, their very similar lives, permeated by the same odd mixture of precocity and ignorance, liberty and restriction, would make it impossible to consider each sister as a separate unit. A laudable wish to steer clear of biography, and a slightly less desirable wish to promote one sister's claims at the expense of the others, has made some critics reluctant to draw comparisons between the work of the three sisters, and the inferior quality of such minor novels as *Agnes Grey* and *The Professor* is another cause of embarrassment. But the minor works are perhaps valuable as guides to the interpretation of the great novels, whose claim to fame can survive the vagaries of critical fashion and the follies of the biographical approach.

It is, however, the literary historians who pose the greatest danger to the reputation of the major Brontë novels. Some of the harshest attacks on Charlotte Brontë came in Cecil's *Early Victorian Novelists* and Leavis's *The Great Tradition*; both these authors admit that Emily is something of a freak in the history of the novel, but the titles of their books do suggest that the Brontës might be considered as early Victorian novelists and as part of a tradition, whereas it is the purpose of this book to show that the Brontës stand right outside any tradition, and cannot be fitted into the history of the nineteenth-century realistic novel. Thomas Hardy, another writer whose works have been attacked for their overblown style, and bedevilled by topographical and biographical speculations, provides the closest parallel to the Brontës, although even he is more closely allied than the Brontës are to the realistic tradition. In reading the Brontës, as well as in reading about their literary education, we must be reminded of parallels with novelists of a different era with very different views on the novel; some of the Brontës' experiments with narrative are suggestive of Proust. Sometimes, especially in *Jane Eyre* and *Wuthering Heights*, where realism seems to have been subordinated to cosmic allegory, we seem to have moved far away from the novel as a genre into the realm of romance. The word romance suggests of course the deterioration of the novel seen as a means of escape from the realities of the world, and it is unfortunate that inferior imitators of the Brontës have brought about this deterioration. But to say that the Brontës are writing romances can mean that we should be comparing their novels with the works of Shakespeare, Spenser, and Sidney, and they can, unlike the great nineteenth-century realist novels, stand this comparison.

NOTES

Chapter One

1. Hewish, *Emily Brontë* (London, 1969), pp. 7–9, states the problem, and Gérin, *Emily Brontë* (Oxford, 1971), pp. 83–84, tries to solve it. Whether Emily was at Law Hill for a short while or over a year is an interesting question because if we knew the answer we would have a little more information about Charlotte's reliability as a witness for her sisters' lives, and about Emily's capacity to live away from home.

2. Except in SHLL., 1, p. 230, Anne is usually assumed to have left home for Thorp Green in March 1841, on the evidence of a letter from Charlotte to Emily of April 2nd, 1841, saying she had heard from Anne. The editors of SHLL. in a footnote to this letter say Anne went to Thorp Green in August 1840, but do not cite any evidence. Mr. Edward Chitham from suggestions in Anne's poetry, especially the poem "Appeal," dated "28.8.1840" in the manuscript, and the evidence of Mr. Robinson's quarterly payments to Anne, has privately informed me that Anne probably left home in May 1840.

3. Date questioned by Knies, *The Art of Charlotte Brontë* (Ohio, 1969), pp. 215–217.

4. Chapple and Pollard, eds., *The Letters of Mrs. Gaskell* (Manchester, 1966), pp. 124, 125, 228, 229.

5. Shorter, *The Brontës: Life and Letters* (London, 1908), Vol. 2, pp. 447–462, and SHLL., 4, pp. 207–214 have useful appendixes listing the letters written by Mr. Nicholls and others to *The Halifax Guardian* and *The Leeds Mercury* when the controversy broke out in 1857. For Charlotte's own evidence see SHLL., 2, pp. 150, 248, and 3, p. 34; also G., p. 64. Additional evidence and opinions are to be found in articles by Weir, "Cowan Bridge: New Light from Old Documents," BST., 56 (1946), pp. 16–28, and Curtis, "Cowan Bridge School: An Old Prospectus Reexamined," BST., 63 (1953), pp. 187–192. Gérin, *Charlotte Brontë: The Evolution of Genius* (Oxford,

1966), pp. 1–16, is a great deal more accurate than Lane, *The Brontë Story* (London, 1953), pp. 42–47.

6. B. Harrison, "The Real Miss Temple," BST., 85 (1975), pp. 361–364, would seem to clear up much of the confusion.

7. Mrs. Gaskell's somewhat difficult relationship with Mr. Brontë is well shown in Chapple and Pollard and in the Penguin edition of Mrs. Gaskell's *Life of Charlotte Brontë* (Harmondsworth, 1975), ed. Shelston, pp. 26–28. Hopkins, *The Father of the Brontës* (Baltimore, 1958), and Lock and Dixon, *A Man of Sorrow* (London, 1965), are sympathetic to their subject, but the recent publication of *Mary Taylor, Friend of Charlotte Brontë: Letters from New Zealand and Elsewhere*, ed. Stevens (Oxford, 1972), shows Mr. Brontë in a very unattractive light, and feminist writers like Peters in *Unquiet Soul* (London, 1975) have caught up with Mr. Brontë's misdemeanours. Pinion, *A Brontë Companion* (London, 1975), pp. 6–25, gives a more balanced view.

8. Miss Branwell's sinister role is taken for granted by most Brontë biographers, although in *The Brontës and their Background* (London, 1973), p. 38, I have tried to put Miss Branwell in perspective. The whole question of the Brontës' religion is a vexed one; even such a scholarly book as Cunningham, *Everywhere Spoken Against: Dissent in the Victorian Novel* (Oxford, 1975), pp. 113–126, following G. E. Harrison, *The Clue to the Brontës* (London, 1948), overstates the Methodist influence on Haworth parsonage.

9. The discovery of Charlotte's letters to Monsieur Heger was a remarkable find, but Spielmann, *The Inner History of the Brontë-Heger Letters* (London, 1919), leaves more questions unanswered than it answers. Subsequent Brontë biographers have been reluctant to guess how many other letters Charlotte wrote, how often and in what tones Monsieur Heger answered, and why and in what circumstances the Heger family first tore up and then preserved the correspondence. Lane, pp. 159–173, shows how Mrs. Gaskell knew about her friend's secret, and how she attempted to conceal it. Sinclair, *The Three Brontës* (London, 1912), pp. 81–90, is an amusing example of pre-Spielmann innocence.

10. The second preserved letter (SHLL., 2, p. 19) asks if Monsieur Heger has heard from Charlotte in May and August 1844, although the first preserved letter was sent in July 1844. The last preserved letter of November 18th, 1845, says Charlotte sent a letter six months earlier, but this has not been preserved.

11. Gérin, *Anne Brontë* (London, 1959), is the most extreme advocate of the hypothesis that Anne was in love with William

Weightman. Apart from *Agnes Grey* the main evidence for this hypothesis is Anne's poetry; the suppression of any autobiographical element in the poems when they were published, although the manuscripts appear to give autobiographical hints, provides some support for the supposed love affair.

12. Du Maurier, *The Infernal World of Branwell Brontë* (London, 1960), does not believe in the affair, but Gérin, *Branwell Brontë* (London, 1961) thinks it authentic. There is a useful discussion of both points of view by Curtis and others in BST., 72 (1962), pp. 3–16. The early account of Leyland, *The Brontë Family: With Special Reference to Patrick Branwell Brontë* (London, 1886), should be treated with caution.

13. Not enough has been written on the Brontës as teachers and governesses; the patient researches of Gérin's books and of numerous writers in BST. have been marred by a readiness to equate fiction with biography, and except in the critical studies of Ewbank, *Their Proper Sphere: A Study of the Brontë Sisters as Early Victorian Novelists* (London, 1966), and of Bjork, *The Language of Truth* (Lund, 1974), there has been little attempt to fit the experiences of the Brontë sisters into a wider nineteenth-century background. Bjork and Ewbank are of course principally interested in the Brontës as women rather than as teachers.

14. G., p. 317.

15. For resemblances between the sisters' novels see Tillotson, *Novels of the Eighteen-Forties* (Oxford, 1954), pp. 285–291, and Andrews, "A Challenge by Anne Brontë," BST., 75 (1965), pp. 29–30.

16. For Branwell's part in the juvenilia see Chapter 3.

17. The question of Branwell's part in *Wuthering Heights* is usually thought to have been settled by Wills, *The Authorship of Wuthering Heights* (London, 1936), but du Maurier, pp. 136–138, shows that the letter of William Dearden to *The Halifax Guardian* in 1867, supported by Grundy, *Pictures of the Past* (London, 1879), and Phillips, "Branwell Brontë," *The Mirror*, December 1872, may have some basis in truth. For an interesting opinion on the authorship of *Wuthering Heights* see Vaisey, "Wuthering Heights," BST., 56 (1946), pp. 15–16.

18. Nussey, "Reminiscences of Charlotte Brontë," *Scribner's Monthly*, May 1871, cited by Hewish, p. 32.

19. Hewish, p. 100. See also Braco, "Emily Brontë's Second Novel," BST., 76 (1966), pp. 28–33.

Chapter Two

1. The most recent work on the juvenilia is Bellour, *Charlotte Brontë: Patrick Branwell Brontë* (Mayenne, 1972). The value of this work is lessened for English readers by the fact that the stories, some of them published for the first time, are translated into French, but in his introduction Bellour gives a fairly scathing account of the speculations launched by previous writers on the juvenilia. He also gives a useful bibliography of previous publications of juvenile stories. Bellour rightly attacks the approach of Gérin, ed., *Five Novelettes* (London, 1971), and Ratchford, *Legends of Angria* (New Haven, 1933) and *The Brontës' Web of Childhood* (New York, 1941), although it is from these books and Bentley's selection of *Tales from Angria* in the Collins edition of *The Professor* (London, 1954) that most students of the Brontës gain their knowledge of the juvenilia. All three writers in their commentary on the juvenilia stress the literary merit of the tales they select, and strive to find literary and biographical parallels. The more comprehensive and less hypothetical Shakespeare Head edition by Wise and Symington of *The Miscellaneous and Unpublished Writings of Charlotte and Branwell Brontë* (Oxford, 1936–1938), and *The Twelve Adventurers and Other Stories* (London, 1925), edited by Shorter and Hatfield, are difficult to get hold of, but between them they print enough of the juvenilia to satisfy all but the most dedicated.

2. For one of these fragments, perhaps written before 1839, see BST., 50 (1940), pp. 15–24, and the discussions in Ratchford, *The Brontës' Web of Childhood*, pp. 101–102, 208–209, and Tillotson, pp. 274–275. For Charlotte's three later fragments, not connected with Angria, *The Moores, Willie Ellin*, and *Emma* see Pinion, pp. 154–157.

3. For the Roe Head Journal in the Brontë Parsonage Museum see Gérin, *Charlotte Brontë: The Evolution of Genius*, pp. 93–105. Charlotte's farewell to Angria is to be found in BST., 34 (1924), p. 229, and Ratchford, *Legends of Angria*, pp. 315–316. Duthie, *The Foreign Vision of Charlotte Brontë* (London, 1975), gives a very useful insight into the extent to which Monsieur Heger as a teacher contributed to the taming of Charlotte's Angrian fantasies.

4. For a new text of this part of the story see Cunningham, pp. 287–291.

5. See Winnifrith, *The Brontës and their Background*, pp. 15–18.

6. *Five Novelettes*, pp. 20–22, and *The Brontës' Web of Childhood*, pp. 189–247. Charlotte in her mature novels is a little ambiva-

lent towards characters like the unregenerate Rochester, Robert Moore, and John Graham, and we can see traces of Zamorna here as well as of Charlotte's feeling that it was wrong to give way to her imagination.

Chapter Three

1. Winnifrith, *The Brontës and their Background*, pp. 15–18, 196. There is still no satisfactory edition of Charlotte's or Anne's poetry, the Shakespeare Head editions, SHCBP. and SHEA., being both inaccurate and inaccessible, although more reliable than earlier editions by Shorter of the three sisters' poems. Hatfield, *The Complete Poems of Emily Jane Brontë* (Oxford, 1941), by comparison is a model of accuracy, but cannot be relied upon completely.

2. The division by Emily of her work into two notebooks, one of which was entitled *Gondal Poems*, has suggested such a dichotomy, but those who wish to emphasise the importance of Gondal, like Ratchford, *Gondal's Queen* (Austin, 1955), deny the importance of the division, and those who think the importance of Gondal is exaggerated can find subjective elements in Gondal poems.

3. SHLL., 1, p. 124.

4. First published in BST., 61 (1951), p. 15.

5. SHLL., 1, pp. 238–239.

6. SHLL., 2, pp. 49–50.

7. SHLL., 2, pp. 52–53.

8. See *Gondal's Queen*, pp. 18, 195.

9. Spark and Stanford, *Emily Brontë, Her Life and Work* (London, 1953), p. 121.

10. The description of the discovery is to be found in the introduction to the 1850 edition of *Wuthering Heights* (WH., p. xliv).

11. Pertinent objections to the reconstruction in *Gondal's Queen* have been made by Paden, *An Investigation of Gondal* (New York, 1958). The three poems on which Ratchford bases her theory are to be found in H., pp. 85, 137, 126.

12. Apart from Pinion, pp. 88–92, and a few biographers there is almost no discussion of Charlotte's verse.

13. SHLL., 1, p. 155.

14. SHLL., 2, pp. 180–181.

15. This point is made by Pinion, p. 92.

16. Harrison and Stanford, *Anne Brontë: Her Life and Work* (London, 1959), and Gérin, *Anne Brontë*, regard the poems as largely autobiographical; there are more discerning comments in Ewbank, pp. 49–52, and Pinion, pp. 230–235.

17. She copied six of them into her manuscript music book, now in the Brontë Parsonage Museum.

18. Harrison and Stanford, p. 172, declare that there are eight Gondal poems written by Anne, but over twenty appear to have at least one Gondal feature.

19. See Chitham, "Almost like Twins," BST., 85 (1975), pp. 365–373.

20. Spark and Stanford, p. 121, say that Emily's major poems are six in number. Hewish, p. 77, names five poems "by which Emily Brontë is known," of which two are not in Spark's selection. Donoghue, "The Other Emily," in *The Brontës: A Collection of Critical Essays*, ed. Gregor (Englewood Cliffs, 1970), pp. 167–168 gives a more representative twenty-four.

21. This poem is well discussed by F. R. Leavis, "Reality and Sincerity: Notes in the Analysis of Poetry," *Scrutiny*, 19 (1952–1953), pp. 90–98.

22. Hewish, pp. 81–83, and Visick, *The Genesis of Wuthering Heights* (Hong Kong, 1958), pp. 35–38.

23. There is thus a textual uncertainty in the fourth stanza from the end, where the missing Honresfeld manuscript, reproduced unsatisfactorily in SHEA., pp. 374–375, might be able to decide between the version of Hatfield, which reads rather awkwardly "And even," and the version of Henderson in *The Complete Poems of Emily Brontë* (London, 1951), which reads "And ever."

24. Notably Gérin, *Emily Brontë*, pp. 243–249.

25. Hewish, pp. 92–93, 109–117, is sceptical of alleged links between the poems and *Wuthering Heights*, but numerous attempts have been made to relate the two. Obviously the Gondal poems include fierce characters like Heathcliff and Catherine and gentle characters like Edgar Linton, and obviously the poems, like *Wuthering Heights*, express extremes of emotion, with perhaps the closest resemblances occurring between some of the latest poems and Heathcliff's moments of rapture as he approaches death. But some of the efforts of Visick, Gérin, and Ratchford to draw parallels between individual poems and particular scenes in *Wuthering Heights* are crude and strained. A more subtle general approach is to be found in Ewbank, pp. 86–155, Miller, *The Disappearance of God* (Harvard, 1963), pp. 151–211, and in articles by Buchen, "Emily Brontë and the Metaphysics of Childhood and Love," NCF., 22 (1967), pp. 63–70, and Davis, "A Reading of *Wuthering Heights*," EC., 19 (1969), pp. 254–272.

Chapter Four

1. Hewish, pp. 91–94, and Gérin, pp. 188–191, give most of the available evidence, although they both think that the length of *Wuthering Heights* may point to the novel being begun earlier than 1845. Charlotte says (SHLL., 2, p. 154) that the proofs of *Wuthering Heights* were ready by August 1847, and her complaints about the procrastination of Newby suggest that Anne and Emily had delivered the manuscript well before that date. If this is so the story that Anne and Emily were busy writing during the summer of 1847, mentioned by Chadwick, *In the Footsteps of the Brontës* (London, 1914), p. 311, is unlikely to refer to *Wuthering Heights*.

2. Allott, *The Brontës: The Critical Heritage* (London, 1974), pp. 28–33, does much to remedy the popular belief that *Wuthering Heights* was totally ignored in the nineteenth century, but admits that nineteenth-century critics found the book confusing.

3. Sanger, *The Structure of Wuthering Heights* (London, 1926).

4. Hafley, "The Villain in *Wuthering Heights*," NCF., 13 (1958–1959), pp. 199–215.

5. The main articles on Lockwood are by Brick, "Wuthering Heights: Narrators, Audience and Message," *College English*, 21 (1959), pp. 80–86, and Woodring, "The Narrators of *Wuthering Heights*," NCF., 11 (1956–1957), pp. 298–305.

6. For conflicting interpretations of the dreams see Van Ghent, "The Window Figure and the Two-Children Figure in *Wuthering Heights*," NCF., 7 (1952–1953), pp. 189–197, and Shannon, "Lockwood's Dreams and the Exegesis of *Wuthering Heights*," NCF., 14 (1959–1960), pp. 95–109.

7. For the best explanation of the reasons for this confusion see Kermode, *The Classic* (London, 1975), which points out that the elder Catherine Earnshaw thinks of becoming Catherine Heathcliff and ends up as Catherine Linton, while the younger Catherine Linton becomes Catherine Heathcliff and ends up as Catherine Earnshaw.

8. In addition to the articles cited in notes 4 and 5, see Mathison, "Nelly Dean and the Power of *Wuthering Heights*," NCF., 11 (1956–1957), pp. 106–129.

9. Even Hewish, p. 150, appears to believe the possibility that Heathcliff may be Catherine's half-brother, and he also suggests that Cathy may be Heathcliff's daughter. A considerable number of articles following Solomon, "The Incest Theme in *Wuthering Heights*," NCF., 14 (1959–1960), pp. 80–83, appear to take incest for granted without weighing the evidence.

10. Craik, *The Brontë Novels* (London, 1968), p. 36.

11. Notably Cecil, *Early Victorian Novelists* (London, 1934), slightly modified in "Fresh Thoughts on the Brontës," BST., 83 (1973), pp. 169–176.

12. Hardy, *Wuthering Heights* (Oxford, 1963), pp. 81–94, defends Isabella.

13. For a good analysis of this passage see Goodridge, *Wuthering Heights* (London, 1964), pp. 32–33.

14. A definite preference for Wuthering Heights over Thrushcross Grange is shown by Q. D. Leavis in *Lectures in America* (London, 1969), and Eagleton, *Myths of Power* (London, 1975). In *The Brontës and their Background*, pp. 189–194, I have argued too dogmatically in favour of Wuthering Heights.

15. Allott, "*Wuthering Heights*: The Rejection of Heathcliff?," EC., 8 (1958), pp. 27–47, is much the best analysis of the problem, although it sees the move to Thrushcross Grange too definitely as a defeat for Heathcliff.

16. Q. D. Leavis, pp. 102–103; Eagleton, p. 117.

17. Cecil defines Hareton and Cathy rather oddly as the children of love. For the interwoven family trees of the Brontës' friends see Stevens, *Mary Taylor, Friend of Charlotte Brontë: Letters from New Zealand and Elsewhere*, pp. 149–155.

18. Ewbank, p. 140; Kermode, pp. 119–120.

19. The most extreme attacks on Heathcliff are by Spark and Stanford, pp. 251–256; for a fine defence of Heathcliff, albeit with some Marxist undertones, see Kettle, *An Introduction to the English Novel*, Vol. 1 (London, 1951), pp. 138–154.

20. There are good surveys of Brontë criticism in the chapters by Christian in *Victorian Fiction: A Guide to Research*, ed. Stevenson (Cambridge, Mass., 1964), and Allott in *The English Novel: Select Bibliographical Guides*, ed. Dyson (Oxford, 1974), although neither survey, nor the earlier article by Watson, "*Wuthering Heights* and the Critics," *The Trollopian*, 3 (1948–1949), pp. 243–263, can keep up with the immense interest in *Wuthering Heights* shown in critical journals, especially NCF. and BST. The collections of articles on *Wuthering Heights* by Allott, Everitt, and Petit are useful. In addition to the works cited in previous notes there are interesting articles by Bradner, "The Growth of *Wuthering Heights*," PMLA., 48 (1933), pp. 129–146; Klingopulos, "The Novel as Dramatic Poem," *Scrutiny*, 14 (1946–1947), pp. 269–286; Watson, "Tempest in the Soul: The Theme and Structure of *Wuthering Heights*," NCF., 4 (1949–1950), pp. 87–100; Traversi, "*Wuthering Heights* after a Hundred Years,"

Dublin Review, 445 (1949), pp. 154–168; Buckley, "Passion and Control in *Wuthering Heights*," *Southern Review*, 1 (1964), pp. 5–23; Jordan, "The Ironic Vision of Emily Brontë," NCF., 20 (1965–1966), pp. 1–18, Hagan; "Control of Sympathy in *Wuthering Heights*," NCF., 21 (1966–1967), pp. 305–323; and Trickett, "*Wuthering Heights*: The Story of a Haunting," BST., 85 (1975), pp. 338–347. Books both on the Brontës in general and on Emily in particular are generally disappointing when they come to a discussion of *Wuthering Heights*.

21. *The Common Reader*, first series (London, 1925), p. 225.

Chapter Five

1. Moore, *Conversations in Ebury Street* (London, 1930), pp. 219–223, is a somewhat lonely voice. Gérin, *Anne Brontë*, and Harrison and Stanford, *Anne Brontë: Her Life and Work*, are largely biographical and there is more of value in Ewbank and Craik. Even BST. has little to say in praise of *Agnes Grey*; Schofield, "The Gentle Anne," BST., 81 (1971), pp. 1–10, is fairly typical of an approach that is both sentimental and condescending. There are some useful points in Hale, *Anne Brontë: Her Life and Writings* (Bloomington, Ind., 1929).

2. For the history of the publication of *Agnes Grey* see SHLL., 2, pp. 52, 87; 4, pp. 315.

3. Craik, pp. 204–205.

4. These remarks are to be found in Anne's preface to TWH., p. xxii, and a letter from Charlotte to W. S. Williams (SHLL., 2, p. 162). Mrs. Gaskell describes a conversation with Charlotte about *Agnes Grey* (G., p. 171) in which the novel is said to be one in which "Anne pretty literally describes her own experiences as a governess."

5. For a good account of this aspect of Mrs. Gaskell's work see Beer, *"Reader, I Married Him"* (London, 1974), pp. 127–174.

6. Craik, p. 215. See also Tillotson, pp. 288–293, for suggestions that *Agnes Grey* influenced *Jane Eyre*.

7. *The Atlas*, January 22nd, 1848, in Allott, *The Brontës: The Critical Heritage*, p. 232. Contemporary reviewers largely ignored *Agnes Grey*.

Chapter Six

1. WH., p. xlviii.
2. Winnifrith, *The Brontës and their Background*, pp. 116–120.
3. SHLL., 2, p. 224.
4. See Chapter 1, note 15. For *The Tenant of Wildfell Hall* as being in some sense an antidote to *Wuthering Heights* see Chitham, "Almost Like Twins."
5. TWH., p. xxii.
6. Winnifrith, *The Brontës and their Background*, pp. 186–189. Eagleton, pp. 128–136, argues quite well that there is a certain amount of irony in the portrait of Markham as a gentleman farmer, and that the account of life at Grassdale succeeds because Helen is as much of an outsider in Huntingdon's circle as Anne would have been.
7. Hargreaves, "Incomplete Texts of *The Tenant of Wildfell Hall*," BST., 82 (1972), pp. 113–117.
8. There are obvious parallels with *The Professor*, where William Crimsworth is clumsy in the same way.
9. This is disputed by Pinion, pp. 254–258, who praises Anne's inventiveness, imagination, and dramatic skill. But it is only on the narrative level that Anne succeeds.
10. The warmest praise for Anne's work is in Craig Bell, *Anne Brontë: The Tenant of Wildfell Hall: A Study and Reappraisal* (Ilkley, 1974), but Pinion, Craik, and the two specialist books on Anne Brontë by Gérin and Harrison and Stanford all praise the novel on this score.
11. Sinclair, p. 54.

Chapter Seven

1. Brammer, "The Manuscript of *The Professor*," RES., N.S. 9 (1960), pp. 157–170, gives most of the facts about *The Professor's* publication. See also SHLL., 2, pp. 140, 161; 3, pp. 206–207; 4, p. 209. Tillotson, p. 280, suggests that *The Professor* was begun seriously at the beginning of 1846 at the end of Charlotte's correspondence with Monsieur Heger, but that its incubation may have taken longer.
2. Chapple and Pollard, p. 409.
3. Hinkley, *The Brontës: Charlotte and Emily* (London, 1947), p. 187, and Pinion, p. 104.

4. Lane, p. 252; Gérin, *Charlotte Brontë: The Evolution of Genius*, pp. 313–316.

5. SHLL., 2, p. 161. But see note 8. Tillotson, pp. 282–283, and Watson, "Form and Substance in the Brontë Novels," in *From Jane Austen to Joseph Conrad*, ed. Rathburn and Steinmann (Minneapolis, 1958), condemn *The Professor's* false start.

6. P., p. xv.

7. See Martin, *The Accents of Persuasion* (London, 1966), pp. 37–38; Knies, p. 93; Pinion, pp. 101–102. A defence of Charlotte's use of French is given by Duthie, pp. 175–198, and more sympathetic accounts of *The Professor* are to be found in Craik, pp. 48–69, and Dessner, *The Homely Web of Truth* (The Hague, 1975), pp. 49–63. It is true that Charlotte can occasionally make a point by the use of French. The position of the adjective in "Votre dévouée élève," as Mr. Martin Wright has pointed out to me, is surely significant.

8. Dessner, p. 50. Charlotte's criticism of the beginning of her novel in 1847 may have caused this revision in 1851.

9. Dessner, pp. 54–57.

10. Notably in *Villette* with the portrait of Cleopatra, although both Mrs. Rochester and Blanche Ingram are strapping women. If *Villette* is in some way a reworking of *The Professor*, the two loves of Lucy Snowe, the handsome John Bretton and the intellectual companion, Paul Emanuel, appear in rather a different light than usually assumed when compared with Mademoiselle Reuter and Frances Henri.

11. Dessner, p. 57.

12. SHLL., 2, p. 161.

Chapter Eight

1. The fluctuations in *Jane Eyre's* reputation are well charted by Christian in *Victorian Fiction* and by Allott in her introduction to the Macmillan casebook on *Jane Eyre* and *Villette* (London, 1973). For F. R. Leavis's remarks see *The Great Tradition* (London, 1948), p. 27, although he does come fairly close to Cecil, *Early Victorian Novelists*, p. 125, when he admits that Charlotte has a permanent interest of a minor kind. Since 1973 there have been published favourable reappraisals of *Jane Eyre* by Eagleton, Bjork, and Dessner in addition to the earlier sympathetic studies by Ewbank, Martin, Knies, and Craik. The preface by Q. D. Leavis in the Penguin *Jane*

Eyre (Harmondsworth, 1966) would seem to mark an important reappraisal.

2. Cross, J. W., *George Eliot's Life as Related in Her Letters and Journals* (London, 1885), 1, p. 306.

3. G., p. 314; SHLL., 2, p. 141. But see my chapter 1, note 3.

4. G., pp. 71, 127, 337, 445, etc. Ray, ed., *The Letters and Private Papers of W. M. Thackeray* (Oxford, 1946), 2, p. 612. The archetypal source for the school of biographical criticism is Wroot, *The Persons and Places in the Brontë Novels* (Shipley, 1935), a misleading and inaccurate work.

5. See Q. D. Leavis in the preface to the Penguin *Jane Eyre*.

6. See Lodge, "Fire and Eyre: Charlotte Brontë's War of Earthly Elements," in *The Language of Fiction* (London, 1961), pp. 114–143, Burkhart; "Another Key Word for *Jane Eyre*," NCF., 16 (1961), pp. 177–179; Ericksen, "Imagery as Structure in *Jane Eyre*" VN., 30 (1966), pp. 18–22; Solomon, "*Jane Eyre*: Fire and Water," *College English*, 25 (1963), pp. 215–217; Heilman, "Charlotte Brontë: Reason and the Moon," NCF., 14 (1960), pp. 283–302.

7. Very different interpretations of the pictures are given by Langford, "The Three Pictures in *Jane Eyre*," VN., 31 (1967), pp. 47–48; by Moser, "From Portrait to Person: A Note on the Surrealistic in *Jane Eyre*," NCF., 20 (1965–1966), pp. 275–281; and by Millgate, "Narrative Distance in *Jane Eyre*: The Relevance of the Pictures," MLR., 63 (1968), pp. 315–319.

8. Heilman, "Charlotte Brontë's New Gothic," in *From Jane Austen to Joseph Conrad*, ed. Rathburn and Steinmann, pp. 118–132.

9. Haight, ed., *The George Eliot Letters* (New Haven, 1954), 1, p. 268.

10. Peters, *Charlotte Brontë: Style in the Novel* (Wisconsin, 1973), pp. 58–66.

11. Most notably by Mrs. Humphry Ward in her preface to the Haworth edition of *Jane Eyre* and by Cecil, *Early Victorian Novelists*.

12. For a valuable defence of Charlotte on this point see Scargill, "All Passion Spent: A Revaluation of *Jane Eyre*," *University of Toronto Quarterly*, 19 (1949), pp. 120–125.

13. Tillotson, p. 310; Martin, p. 87.

14. SHLL., 3, p. 328. See Winnifrith, *The Brontës and their Background*, pp. 54–56.

15. Cunningham maintains that almost all Victorian novelists are unfair to Evangelicals and Dissenters.

16. Eagleton, pp. 27–29.

Chapter Nine

1. The story of *Shirley*'s publication can be found in G., pp. 413–435, and Gérin, *Charlotte Brontë: The Evolution of Genius*, pp. 389–413. The relevant letters from Charlotte to her publishers are in SHLL., 2, pp. 161, 189, 305, 306, and 3, pp. 13–17, 25, although we would know more about the novel if we had access to the full correspondence between George Smith and Charlotte, mentioned in BST., 84 (1974), pp. 310–311, and 85 (1975), p. 420. Dr. H. J. Rosengarten in an unpublished Cambridge Ph.D. thesis suggests that *The Moores* may be a false start by Charlotte when working on *Shirley*, although it is usually dated before *The Professor*.

2. Rosengarten gives a full, if slightly unsympathetic account of contemporary reviews of *Shirley*, on which see also Allott, *The Brontës: The Critical Heritage*, pp. 117–170, and Winnifrith, *The Brontës and their Background*, pp. 123–128.

3. The recent publication in the Penguin English library of *Shirley*, ed. by A. and J. Hook (Harmondsworth, 1974), with a spirited defence of the novel's unity and originality, may indicate an upsurge of interest in *Shirley*. Dr. Rosengarten as well as establishing the definitive text of *Shirley* has some very full explanatory notes, and an excellent historical introduction. There are chapters on *Shirley* in the books by Martin, Craik, Knies, Pinion, and Dessner, but these do little to further the novel's reputation.

4. Stevens has much helpful information about the East Yorkshire background, but her work, like that of other biographers, blurs fact and fiction.

5. For the debate on the original of Caroline Helstone see Spens, "Charlotte Brontë," *Essays and Studies by Members of the English Association*, 14 (1929), pp. 54–70; Tompkins, "Caroline Helstone's Eyes," BST., 71 (1961), pp. 18–28; and Holgate, "The Structure of *Shirley*," BST., 72 (1962), pp. 27–35.

6. Briggs, "Private and Social Themes in *Shirley*," BST., 68 (1958), pp. 203–219, establishes Charlotte's historical accuracy, and Eagleton, pp. 45–60, does something to evaluate Charlotte as a social critic.

7. For the anecdote by Francis Butterfield of Wilsden that Charlotte originally intended to write about Chartism see Holgate, p. 29.

8. This point is made in the introduction to the Penguin *Shirley*, p. 25.

9. BST., 85 (1975), pp. 329–337, has now published the full text of *A Word to the Quarterly* and comments on the resemblances between *Shirley* and Lady Eastlake's review.

10. There are some good insights into *Shirley* as a feminist novel in Ewbank, Korg, and, more provokingly, in Eagleton and in Beer, pp. 84–126.

11. Only the Hooks, Korg, "The Problem of Unity in *Shirley*," NCF., 12 (1957–1958), pp. 125–136, and Shapiro, "Public Themes and Private Lives: Social Criticism in *Shirley*," *Papers on Language and Literature*, 4 (1968), pp. 74–84, have really attempted to explore the links between the various strands in *Shirley*.

12. Knies, pp. 158–162, and Dessner, pp. 82–97, are rightly critical of Charlotte's change in narrative method.

Chapter Ten

1. Winnifrith, *The Brontës and their Background*, pp. 128–132. Allott, *The Brontës: The Critical Heritage*, pp. 171–215.

2. Allott, *The Brontës: The Critical Heritage*, pp. 383, 415, 428, 445, for some late Victorian comments.

3. SHLL., 3, pp. 207, 293, 295, 297, 323; 4, pp. 1–40.

4. As announced in BST., 84 (1974), p. 310, fifteen unpublished letters were given to the Brontë Parsonage Museum by George Smith's granddaughter, but these have not been published.

5. This point, backed up by some comments on Charlotte's perverse style, is well made by Peters, *Charlotte Brontë: Style in the Novel*, pp. 58–66.

6. V., p. 350. This is another link between John Bretton and St. John Rivers, a resemblance noted but not stressed by Martin, p. 172, n. 1.

7. There is a sensible discussion of this scene in Bjork, pp. 63–64, and a less sensible one in Eagleton, p. 70.

8. See Dessner, pp. 103–110.

9. In addition to the standard works on Charlotte Brontë there are interesting but divergent articles on *Villette* by Heilman, "Charlotte Brontë, Reason and the Moon," NCF., 14 (1959–1960), pp. 283–302; Johnson, " 'Daring the Dread Glance': Charlotte Brontë's Treatment of the Supernatural in *Villette*," NCF., 20 (1965–1966), pp. 325–336; and by Colby, *Fiction with a Purpose: Major and Minor Nineteenth-Century Novels* (London, 1967), pp. 178–212.

10. SHLL., 4, pp. 16, 18, 54.

11. Ratchford, *The Brontës' Web of Childhood*, p. 240.

12. The rudeness about Belgium, noted by Dunbar, "Proper Names in *Villette*," NCF., 14 (1959–1960), pp. 77–80, is hardly subtle.

13. Colby, "*Villette* and the Life of the Mind," PMLA., 85 (1960), pp. 410–419.

SELECT BIBLIOGRAPHY

Allott, M., "*Wuthering Heights*: The Rejection of Heathcliff?" *Essays in Criticism*, 8 (1958), pp. 27–47.

——, *Emily Brontë: Wuthering Heights*, Casebook Series (London, 1970).

——, *Charlotte Brontë: Jane Eyre and Villette*, Casebook Series (London, 1973).

——, *The Brontës: The Critical Heritage* (London, 1974).

——, "The Brontës," in *The English Novel: Select Bibliographical Guides*, edited by A. E. Dyson (Oxford, 1974).

Andrews, W. L., "A Challenge by Anne Brontë," *Brontë Society Transactions*, 75 (1965), pp. 25–30.

Beer, P., "*Reader, I Married Him*": *A Study of the Woman Characters of Jane Austen, Charlotte Brontë, Elizabeth Gaskell and George Eliot* (London, 1974).

Bellour, R., *Charlotte Brontë: Patrick Branwell Brontë* (Mayenne, 1972).

Bentley, P., *The Brontës* (London, 1947).

——, *The Brontës and Their World* (London, 1969).

Bjork, H., *The Language of Truth* (Lund, 1974).

Blondel, J., *Emily Brontë: Expérience Spirituelle et Création Poétique* (Paris, 1955).

Braco, E. J., "Emily Brontë's Second Novel," *Brontë Society Transactions*, 76 (1966), pp. 28–33.

Bradby, G. F., *The Brontës and Other Essays* (Oxford, 1932).

Bradner, L., "The Growth of Wuthering Heights," *Publications of the Modern Language Association*, 48 (1933), pp. 129–146.

Brammer, M. M., "The Manuscript of *The Professor*," *Review of English Studies*, N.S. 9 (1960), pp. 157–170.

Brick, A. R., "Wuthering Heights: Narrators, Audience and Message," *College English*, 21 (1959), pp. 80–86.

Briggs, A., "Private and Social Themes in *Shirley*," *Brontë Society Transactions*, 68 (1958), pp. 203–219.

Brontë family, *The Life and Works of Charlotte Brontë and Her Sisters*, Haworth edition, 7 volumes. Edited by Mrs. H. Ward and C. K. Shorter (London, 1899–1900).

——, *The Shakespeare Head Brontë*, 19 volumes. Edited by T. J. Wise and J. A. Symington (Oxford, 1931–1938).

Brontë, C., *The Twelve Adventurers and Other Stories*. Edited by C. K. Shorter and C. W. Hatfield (London, 1925).

——, *Legends of Angria: Compiled from the Early Writings of Charlotte Brontë*. Edited by F. E. Ratchford and W. C. de Vane (New Haven, 1933).

——, *The Professor*. Edited by P. Bentley (London, 1954).

——, *Jane Eyre*. Edited by Q. D. Leavis (Harmondsworth, 1966).

——, *Jane Eyre*. Edited by J. Jack and M. Smith (Oxford, 1969).

——, *Five Novelettes: Passing Events, Julia, Mina Laury, Captain Henry Hastings, Caroline Vernon*. Transcribed and edited by W. Gérin (London, 1971).

——, *Shirley*. Edited by A. and J. Hook (Harmondsworth, 1974).

Brontë, E. J., *The Complete Poems of Emily Jane Brontë*. Edited by C. W. Hatfield (Oxford, 1941).

——, *The Complete Poems of Emily Brontë*. Edited by P. Henderson (London, 1951).

Buchen, I. H., "Emily Brontë and the Metaphysics of Childhood and Love," *Nineteenth-Century Fiction*, 22 (1967), pp. 63–70.

Buckley, V., "Passion and Control in *Wuthering Heights*," *Southern Review* (Sydney), I (1964), pp. 5–23.

Burkhart, C., "Another Key Word for *Jane Eyre*," *Nineteenth-Century Fiction*, 16 (1961), pp. 177–179.

——, *Charlotte Brontë: A Psychosexual Study of Her Novels* (London, 1973).

Cecil, D., *Early Victorian Novelists: Essays in Revaluation* (London, 1934).

——, "Fresh Thoughts on the Brontës," *Brontë Society Transactions*, 83 (1973), pp. 169–176.

Chadwick, E. A., *In the Footsteps of the Brontës* (London, 1914).

Chase, R., "The Brontës: A Centennial Observance," *Kenyon Review*, 9 (1947), pp. 487–506.

Chitham, E., "Almost Like Twins," *Brontë Society Transactions*, 85 (1975), pp. 365–373.

Christian, M., "The Brontës," *Victorian Fiction: A Guide to Research.* Edited by L. Stevenson (Cambridge, Mass., 1964).

Colby, R. A., "*Villette* and the Life of the Mind," *Publications of the Modern Language Association,* 85 (1960), pp. 410–419.

——, *Fiction with a Purpose: Major and Minor Nineteenth-Century Novels* (London, 1967).

Craig Bell, A., *Anne Brontë: The Tenant of Wildfell Hall: A Study and Reappraisal* (Ilkley, 1974).

Craik, W. A., *The Brontë Novels* (London, 1968).

Crompton, D. W., "The New Criticism: A Caveat," *Essays in Criticism,* 10 (1960), pp. 359–364.

Cross, J. W., *George Eliot's Life as Related in Her Letters and Journals* (London, 1885).

Cunningham, V. W., *Everywhere Spoken Against: Dissent in the Victorian Novel* (Oxford, 1975).

Curtis, M., "Cowan Bridge School: An Old Prospectus Reexamined," *Brontë Society Transactions,* 63 (1953), pp. 187–192.

—— et al., "Further Thoughts on Branwell Brontë's Story: A Discussion," *Brontë Society Transactions,* 72 (1962), pp. 3–16.

Davies, C. W., "A Reading of *Wuthering Heights,*" *Essays in Criticism,* 19 (1969), pp. 254–273.

Dessner, L. J., *The Homely Web of Truth* (The Hague, 1975).

Drew, P., "Charlotte Brontë as a Critic of *Wuthering Heights,*" *Nineteenth-Century Fiction,* 18 (1963–1964), pp. 365–381.

Dry, F. S., *The Sources of Wuthering Heights* (Cambridge, 1937).

——, *The Sources of Jane Eyre* (Cambridge, 1940).

Dunbar, G., "Proper Names in *Villette,*" *Nineteenth-Century Fiction,* 14 (1959–1960), pp. 77–80.

Duthie, E. L., *The Foreign Vision of Charlotte Brontë* (London, 1975).

Eagleton, T., *Myths of Power: A Marxist Study of the Brontës* (London, 1975).

Eliot, G., *The George Eliot Letters.* Six volumes. Edited by G. S. Haight (New Haven, 1954).

Ericksen, D. N., "Imagery as Structure in *Jane Eyre,*" *Victorian Newsletter,* 30 (1966), pp. 215–217.

Everitt, A., *Wuthering Heights: An Anthology of Criticism* (London, 1967).

Ewbank, I-S., *Their Proper Sphere: A Study of the Brontë Sisters as Early Victorian Female Novelists* (London, 1966).

Gaskell, E. C., *The Letters of Mrs. Gaskell.* Edited by J. A. V. Chapple and A. E. Pollard (Manchester, 1966).

——, *The Life of Charlotte Brontë*. Edited by A. Shelston (Harmondsworth, 1975).

Gérin, W., *Anne Brontë* (London, 1959). Revised edition (London, 1975).

——, *Branwell Brontë* (London, 1961).

——, *Charlotte Brontë: The Evolution of Genius* (Oxford, 1966).

——, *Emily Brontë* (Oxford, 1971).

Goodridge, F. W., *Wuthering Heights* (London, 1964).

Gose, E. B., "Wuthering Heights: The Heath and the Hearth," *Nineteenth-Century Fiction*, 21 (1966–1967), pp. 1–18.

Gregor, I., ed., *The Brontës: A Collection of Critical Essays* (Englewood Cliffs, 1970).

Grundy, F., *Pictures of the Past* (London, 1879).

Hafley, J., "The Villain in *Wuthering Heights*," *Nineteenth-Century Fiction*, 13 (1958–1959), pp. 199–215.

Hagan, J., "Control of Sympathy in *Wuthering Heights*," *Nineteenth-Century Fiction*, 21 (1966–1967), pp. 305–323.

Hale, W. T., *Anne Brontë: Her Life and Writings* (Bloomington, Ind., 1929).

Hanson, L. and E. M., *The Four Brontës* (Oxford, 1949). Revised edition (Hamden, Conn., 1967).

Hardy, B., *Wuthering Heights*. Notes on English Literature (Oxford, 1963).

——, *Jane Eyre*. Notes on English Literature (Oxford, 1964).

Hargreaves, G. D., "Incomplete Texts of *The Tenant of Wildfell Hall*," *Brontë Society Transactions*, 82 (1972), pp. 113–117.

Harrison, A., and Stanford, D., *Anne Brontë: Her Life and Work* (London, 1959).

Harrison, B., "The Real Miss Temple," *Brontë Society Transactions*, 85 (1975), pp. 361–364.

Harrison, G. E., *The Clue to the Brontës* (London, 1948).

Heilman, R. B., "Charlotte Brontë, Reason and the Moon," *Nineteenth-Century Fiction*, 14 (1959–1960), pp. 283–302.

——, "Charlotte Brontë's New Gothic," in *From Jane Austen to Joseph Conrad*. Edited by R. Rathburn and M. Steinmann, Jr. (Minneapolis, 1958).

Hewish, J., *Emily Brontë* (London, 1969).

Hinkley, L., *The Brontës: Charlotte and Emily* (London, 1947).

Holgate, I., "The Structure of *Shirley*," *Brontë Society Transactions*, 72 (1962), pp. 27–35.

Hopkins, A., *Elizabeth Gaskell: Her Life and Work* (London, 1952).

——, *The Father of the Brontës* (Baltimore, 1958).

Johnson, E. D. H., " 'Daring the Dread Glance': Charlotte's Treatment of the Supernatural in *Villette*," *Nineteenth-Century Fiction*, 20 (1965–1966), pp. 325–336.

Jordan, J. E., "The Ironic Vision of Emily Brontë," *Nineteenth-Century Fiction*, 20 (1965–1966), pp. 1–18.

Kermode, F., *The Classic* (London, 1975).

Kettle, A., *An Introduction to the English Novel*, Vol. I (London, 1951).

Klingopulos, G. D., "The Novel as Dramatic Poem (2): *Wuthering Heights*," *Scrutiny*, 14 (1946–1947), pp. 269–286.

Knies, E. A., *The Art of Charlotte Brontë* (Ohio, 1969).

Korg, J., "The Problem of Unity in *Shirley*," *Nineteenth-Century Fiction*, 12 (1957–1958), pp. 125–136.

Lane, M., *The Brontë Story: A Reconsideration of Mrs. Gaskell's Life of Charlotte Brontë* (London, 1953).

Langford, T., "The Three Pictures in *Jane Eyre*," *Victorian Newsletter*, 31 (1967), pp. 47–48.

Langman, F. H., "*Wuthering Heights*," *Essays in Criticism*, 15 (1965), pp. 294–312.

Leavis, F. R., *The Great Tradition* (London, 1948).

——, "Reality and Sincerity: Notes in the Analysis of Poetry," *Scrutiny*, 19 (1952–1953), pp. 90–98.

Leavis, Q. D., "A Fresh Approach to *Wuthering Heights*," in *Lectures in America* by F. R. and Q. D. Leavis (London, 1969).

Leyland, F., *The Brontë Family: With Special Reference to Patrick Branwell Brontë*, 2 volumes (London, 1886).

Lock, J., and Dixon, W. T., *A Man of Sorrow: The Life, Letters and Times of the Rev. Patrick Brontë* (London, 1965).

Lodge, D., "Fire and Eyre: Charlotte Brontë's War of Earthly Elements," in *The Language of Fiction: Essays in Criticism and Verbal Analysis of the English Novel* (London, 1961).

Martin, R., *The Accents of Persuasion: Charlotte Brontë's Novels* (London, 1966).

Mathison, J., "Nelly Dean and the Power of *Wuthering Heights*," *Nineteenth-Century Fiction*, 11 (1956–1957), pp. 106–129.

Maurier, D. du., *The Infernal World of Branwell Brontë* (London, 1960).

McKibben, R. C., "The Image of the Book in *Wuthering Heights*," *Nineteenth-Century Fiction*, 15 (1960), pp. 159–169.

Miller, J. Hillis, "Emily Brontë," in *The Disappearance of God* (Harvard, 1963).

Millgate, J., "Narrative Distance in *Jane Eyre*: The Relevance of the Pictures," *Modern Language Review*, 63 (1968), pp. 315–319.

Moore, G., *Conversations in Ebury Street* (London, 1930).

Moser, L. E., "From Portrait to Person: A Note on the Surrealistic in *Jane Eyre*," *Nineteenth-Century Fiction*, 20 (1965–1966), pp. 275–281.

Nussey, E., "Reminiscences of Charlotte Brontë," *Scribners' Monthly*, May 1871.

Oram, E. A., "A Brief for Miss Branwell," *Brontë Society Transactions*, 74 (1964), pp. 28–38.

Paden, W. D., *An Investigation of Gondal* (New York, 1958).

Peters, M., *Charlotte Brontë: Style in the Novel* (Wisconsin, 1973).

——, *Unquiet Soul: A Biography of Charlotte Brontë* (London, 1975).

Petit, J. F., ed., *Emily Brontë*. Penguin Critical Anthology (Harmondsworth, 1973).

Phillips, G., "Branwell Brontë," *The Mirror*, December 1872.

Pinion, F., *A Brontë Companion* (London, 1975).

Pollard, A. E., *Charlotte Brontë*. Profiles in Literature (London, 1968).

Prescott, J., "*Jane Eyre*: A Romantic Exemplum with a Difference," in *Twelve Original Essays on Great Novelists*. Edited by C. Shapiro (Detroit, 1960).

Ratchford, F. E., *The Brontës' Web of Childhood* (New York, 1941).

——, *Gondal's Queen: A Novel in Verse* (Austin, 1955).

Robinson, A. M. F., *Emily Brontë* (London, 1883).

Sanger, C. P., *The Structure of Wuthering Heights* (London, 1926).

Scargill, M. H., "All Passion Spent: A Revaluation of *Jane Eyre*," *University of Toronto Quarterly*, 19 (1949), pp. 120–125.

Schofield, G., "The Gentle Anne," *Brontë Society Transactions*, 81 (1971), pp. 1–10.

Schorer, M., "Fiction and the 'Analogical Matrix,'" *Kenyon Review*, 11 (1949), pp. 539–560.

Scruton, W., "Reminiscences of the Late Miss Ellen Nussey," *Brontë Society Transactions*, 8 (1898), pp. 23–42.

Shannon, E. F., Jr., "Lockwood's Dreams and the Exegesis of *Wuthering Heights*," *Nineteenth-Century Fiction*, 14 (1959–1960), pp. 95–109.

Shapiro, A., "Public Themes and Private Lives: Social Criticism in *Shirley*," *Papers on Language and Literature*, 4 (1968), pp. 74–84.

Sherry, N., *Charlotte and Emily Brontë* (London, 1970).

Shorter, C. K., *Charlotte Brontë and Her Circle* (London, 1896).

——, *The Brontës: Life and Letters*. Two volumes (London, 1908).

Simpson, C., *Emily Brontë* (London, 1929).

Sinclair, M., *The Three Brontës* (London, 1912).

Solomon, E., "The Incest Theme in *Wuthering Heights*," *Nineteenth-Century Fiction*, 14 (1959–1960), pp. 80–83.

——, "*Jane Eyre*: Fire and Water," *College English*, 25 (1963), pp. 215–217.

Spark, M., and Stanford, D., *Emily Brontë* (London, 1953).

Spens, J., "Charlotte Brontë," *Essays and Studies by Members of the English Association*, 14 (1929), pp. 54–70.

Spielmann, M. H., *The Inner History of the Brontë-Heger Letters* (London, 1919).

Stevens, J., ed., *Mary Taylor, Friend of Charlotte Brontë: Letters from New Zealand and Elsewhere* (Oxford, 1972).

Stevenson, W. E., *Anne and Emily Brontë*. Profiles in Literature (London, 1968).

Sugden, K. A. R., *A Short History of the Brontës* (Oxford, 1929).

Thackeray, W. M., *The Letters and Private Papers of William Makepeace Thackeray*. Edited by G. N. Ray (Oxford, 1946).

Thompson, W., "Infanticide and Sadism in *Wuthering Heights*," *Publications of the Modern Language Association*, 78 (1963).

Tillotson, K., *Novels of the Eighteen-Forties* (Oxford, 1954).

Tompkins, J. M. S., "Caroline Helstone's Eyes," *Brontë Society Transactions*, 71 (1961), pp. 18–28.

——, "*Jane Eyre's* 'Iron Shroud,'" *Modern Language Review*, 22 (1927), pp. 195–197.

Traversi, D., "*Wuthering Heights* after a Hundred Years," *Dublin Review*, 445 (1949), pp. 154–168.

Trickett, R., "*Wuthering Heights*: The Story of a Haunting," *Brontë Society Transactions*, 85 (1975), pp. 338–347.

Vaisey, J., "*Wuthering Heights*," *Brontë Society Transactions*, 56 (1946), pp. 15–16.

Van Ghent, D., "The Window Figure and the Two-Children Figure in *Wuthering Heights*," *Nineteenth-Century Fiction*, 7 (1952–1953), pp. 189–197.

Visick, M., *The Genesis of Wuthering Heights* (Hong Kong, 1958).

Watson, M. R., "*Wuthering Heights* and the Critics," *The Trollopian*, 3 (1948–1949), pp. 243–263.

——, "Tempest in the Soul: The Theme and Structure of *Wuthering Heights*," *Nineteenth-Century Fiction*, 4 (1949–1950), pp. 87–100.

——, "Form and Substance in the Brontë Novels," in *From Jane*

Austen to Joseph Conrad. Edited by R. C. Rathburn and M. Steinmann, Jr. (Minneapolis, 1958).

Weir, E., "Cowan Bridge: New Light from Old Documents," *Brontë Society Transactions*, 56 (1946), pp. 16–28.

Wills, I. C., *The Authorship of Wuthering Heights* (London, 1936).

——, *The Brontës* (London, 1933).

Winnifrith, T. J., *The Brontës and their Background* (London, 1973).

Woodring, C. R., "The Narrators of *Wuthering Heights*," *Nineteenth-Century Fiction*, 11 (1956–1957), pp. 298–305.

Woolf, V., "*Jane Eyre* and *Wuthering Heights*," in *The Common Reader*, first series (London, 1925), pp. 196–205.

Wroot, H. E., *The Persons and Places in the Brontë Novels* (Shipley, 1935).

INDEX